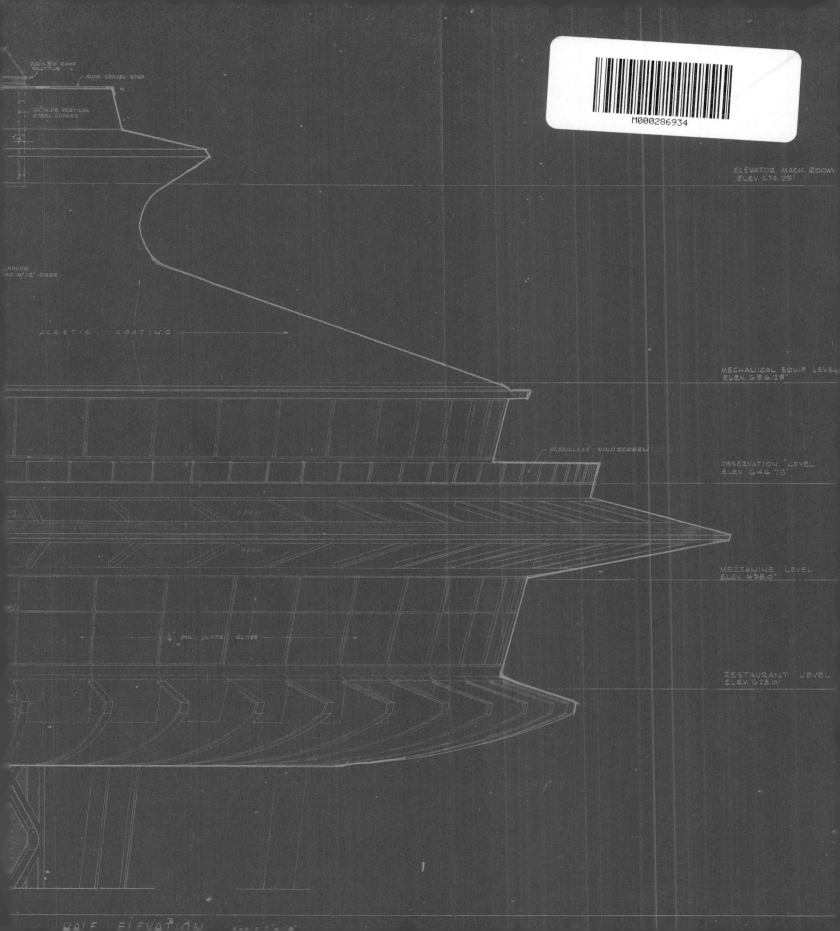

2'0" x 3'0" ROOF
SCUTTLE

ALUM. GRAVEL STOP

12" WIDE VERTICAL
STEEL LADDER

7"

LADDER
40 W/12" RISER

PLASTIC COATING

PLEXIGLASS WIND SCREEN

OPEN

OPEN

1/4" POL. PLATE GLASS

ELEVATOR MACH. ROOM
ELEV. 674.25'

MECHANICAL EQUIP LEVEL
ELEV. 656.25'

OBSERVATION LEVEL
ELEV. 646.75'

MEZZANINE LEVEL
ELEV. 638.0'

RESTAURANT LEVEL
ELEV. 628.0'

HALF ELEVATION

To dreamers, risk takers, and daredevil builders

SPACE NEEDLE

THE SPIRIT OF SEATTLE › KNUTE BERGER

DOCUMENTARY MEDIA LLC

SEATTLE, WASHINGTON

Space Needle: The Spirit of Seattle

Space Needle LLC
203 Sixth Avenue North
Seattle WA 98109
www.spaceneedle.com

Published by Documentary Media LLC
3250 41st Ave SW
Seattle WA 98116
206-935-9292
books@docbooks.com
www.documentarymedia.com

First Edition
Printed in Canada

Author: Knute Berger
Project Manager: Mary Bacarella
Designer: Jon Cannell
Editor: Judy Gouldthorpe
Executive Editor: Barry Provorse
Publisher: Petyr Beck

ISBN: 978-1-933245-25-6 (hard cover)
ISBN: 978-1-933245-26-3 (soft cover)

Library of Congress Cataloging-in-Publication Data:

Berger, Knute, 1953-
Space Needle: the spirit of Seattle / Knute Berger. – 1st ed.
    p. cm.
Includes index.
ISBN 978-1-933245-25-6 (alk. paper)
1. Space Needle (Seattle, Wash.) 2. Space Needle (Seattle, Wash.) – History.
3. Space Needle (Seattle, Wash.) – Anniversaries, etc. 4. Seattle (Wash.) –
History. 5. Seattle (Wash.) – Buildings, structures, etc. I. Title
F899.S48S643 2012
979.7'772–dc23
                2012006986

Contents

Artist Bo Bartlett captures the multigenerational spirit of the Space Needle in his 2006 painting "Father and Son."

Foreword

The Space Needle has been a part of my life as long as I can remember. When I was a preschooler, my father, Howard S. Wright, took me to his company's construction site and up the elevator to the top. I have to admit that I was a little scared, but the impression was indelible. What a view.

Half a century has passed, and as we celebrate the Space Needle's 50th anniversary, I can't help but wonder how the city might be different if my father and community leaders Eddie Carlson, John Graham, Norton Clapp, Ned Skinner, and Bagley Wright had not shared a vision. It began with Eddie's quick sketch of a tower a world away that got them thinking, "Why not here?" Less than two years later, it became the symbol of the Seattle World's Fair, Century 21.

Stewardship of this remarkable structure comes with great responsibility, as the Space Needle has become a physical expression of our city's spirit and a beacon that marks our place in the world. Together, we have celebrated the diversity of our city, the Olympic torch, sports championships, and landmark events and grieved over the tragedies that have touched all our lives. Year after year, the fireworks display on New Year's Eve transports us into the unknown challenges and opportunities of the future. It's been an amazing ride.

No one knew what lay ahead when the Space Needle opened in 1962. It was called the Age of Space, but never could we imagine the realities that would come to be. On behalf of my family, I have to express the strong sense of pride we take in what others have entrusted to us. The incredible legacy of this structure, and all that comes with it, keeps us on the leading edge of creativity, technology, and lifestyle. Whatever the future brings, the Space Needle will be there as the cornerstone for all that is new and exciting in our city and our lives.

Jeff Wright
Chairman
Space Needle, LLC
Seattle, Washington

"With their feet on the ground and their hearts in the sky"

The Space Needle has a kind of totemic power. It is a civic symbol, an international icon, and has deeply personal meanings for many of the people who have visited it or lived in its shadow for the last half-century. It's a place where we mark the events of our lives, from weddings and anniversaries to bar mitzvahs. It has been the site of first dates, celebrity sightings, births, deaths, and world firsts.

It is the symbol of home to millions of people on Puget Sound, the man-made beacon that marks our place. Even more, it embodies the hopes and dreams of an age. It was built in an era of conflict to represent hope. It was constructed at a troubled time to reflect the dream of a better future. It was raised as a gesture to our friends and enemies, letting them know that our destiny lay in a New Frontier.

Its totemic quality was suggested in the 1974 Hollywood thriller *The Parallax View*, which director Alan J. Pakula opened with a shot panning from a North Coast Indian totem pole to the shaft of the Needle. Pakula himself called the Needle "an American totem." In writing about the Needle, you come to understand how much it means to people. Everyone has an experience, an opinion, an artifact, or a bit of family lore to relate. It truly is a tower with power.

While the Needle is personal for many of us, it came into being within a larger context— the Cold War. Indeed, it would not exist but for the Cold War. It was born out of competition with the Soviet Union as a response to the spread of Communism. The Russians launched *Sputnik* into orbit and kicked off the space race in 1957. The Space Needle became a symbol of the American response. It signaled the importance of science to America's future. It was built for a world's fair to reflect the 21st century, a high-tech age of American leadership and vision just over the horizon.

The Needle's spire pointed to the stars, its restaurant revolved like a satellite, the ingenuity, speed, and craft of its designers and builders gave proof of American know-how. The flying-saucer top suggested a future when we would travel between planets, rising above the difficulties of this world to find peace and prosperity in the heavens. We could, someday, up there, be our very best selves. The Needle embodied that dream and pointed the way.

To get a sense of the world that birthed the Needle, all you have to do is leaf through the newspapers of the late 1950s and early 1960s to feel the looming threat and heady potential of the times. The possibility of atomic war was real; the world was in transition and conflicts arose everywhere, from Europe, Africa, and the Middle East to remote places such as Vietnam and next-door neighbors like Cuba. Humans were making their first forays into space. In May 1961, the month when the Space Needle's massive foundation was

In 1961, a statue of the city's namesake, Chief Sealth, seems to reach out to Seattle's still-under-construction Space Age totem, the Space Needle.

poured, astronaut Alan Shepard became the first American to travel into space. It was a time when we were building rockets, but also digging fallout shelters. The pendulum swung between hope and fear, between promise and nuclear annihilation. In some ways, it was almost radical to suggest we *had* a future, let alone a happy one.

In August 1961, the Space Needle was a hive of activity. Skilled and fast-moving ironworkers had just passed the 200-foot level, and people could see the three yellow legs of this strange new structure rising on the flats between downtown and Queen Anne Hill. Crews were working extra shifts as the Needle builders tried to do the seemingly impossible: raise a unique 600-foot tower of steel in a year, something that would be the symbol of the Seattle World's Fair of 1962, themed "Man in the Space Age."

The *Seattle Times* of August 13 provided interesting contrasts. It was a historic date, for it was the day when the Berlin Wall was begun. The Iron Curtain was a symbol of the worst of the Cold War: a world divided, its people viewing each other through barbed wire and along machine-gun sights. That summer Sunday in Seattle, the front-page headline blared: "E. Germans Seal Off West Berlin to Refugees."

At the bottom of the front page was a tiny blurb and picture of the future Space Needle. It happily announced that up to 1.5 million fairgoers would be able to dine in the rotating restaurant of the Needle, now under construction. While East and West faced off in a growing crisis, the American response had made Seattle a kind of ground zero of optimism. Instead of building walls, we were increasing vistas and inviting the world to town to see what Seattle and America could do. While others were hunkering down, we were building up.

The impetus for Century 21's Space Age theme was the space race between the United States and the Soviet Union, reflected in these stamps from 1962.

The Needle was meant to embody the fair's themes, but also send a message to the world that Seattle was the launchpad for reaching the New Frontier, with the Needle pointing the way.

Further into that Sunday newspaper, a headline read, "Colonization of Other Planets Impossible, Says Russ." A Russian scientist pooh-poohed the notion that humans could save themselves by rocketing off to Mars or other stops in the solar system—they were too expensive to reach and not capable of sustaining human life. Our solutions, some scientists believed, would have to be found right here on earth.

That notion took aim at the faddish idea that putting people in space would solve our earthly woes of overcrowding and gobbling up our natural resources. Sobering as the current situation was, however, there was something to the idea of trying to stretch ourselves, to advance technology, to reach out for a better life with the kind of vision and vigor that John F. Kennedy, the new president, admired. Seattle, an American city close to its pioneer roots, was ideally suited to the task. As world's fair scholar Paul Greenhalgh has observed, "the pioneers were rocket-driven" at Space Age fairs like Seattle's.

Space was also a place where international cooperation just might be possible. While the Americans and Soviets vied for domination, there was also a chance that a weightless humankind could shed the gravity of old ways and start afresh.

So the Space Needle became a symbol of those dreams without ever leaving the ground. Among its builders were some who had worked on rocket projects, but the Needle was never designed to lift off. Instead, it was famed for its stability and durability, its solid and deep foundation. The Needle had come to live among us to stand for something, and to do so as a permanent landmark for a long time to come.

There are many personal stories that capture the essence of the Needle. Most Seattleites were standing on the ground in 1961, and looking up as the Needle rose. Some were entranced, almost hypnotized by the process, like Mrs. Ethel M. Lyons, a retired schoolteacher and widow of a Spanish-American War veteran. She rode the bus from her home in the University District to the work site every day, often as early as 5 a.m., to peek through the fence and watch the Needle's progress. The ironworkers dubbed her the Needle's "No. 1 Fan" and "Mother of the Space Needle," and presented her with her own hard hat. She brought the crews Thanksgiving pies and Christmas fruitcakes. Even during the fair, the Needle became an almost daily ritual for Mrs. Lyons.

A lucky few had a chance to be among the first to see the view from high above. In the late fall of 1961, Jeff Wright, now chairman of the company that owns the Space Needle, was a four-year-old boy whose larger-than-life father, Howard S. Wright, was overseeing construction of the tower. He ran a family company that almost literally built the Pacific Northwest we know today, from skyscrapers and malls to Grand Coulee Dam and nuclear plants. On Saturday mornings, Jeff's dad would take him to work sites. One day, they climbed into the open construction elevator with its cyclone fence "walls" and rose 500 feet in the air to the top of Dad's latest project, the Space Needle. Young Jeff clung to his father's legs, scared to death. Tourists still gasp at the ride today, even from inside cozy modern elevators. The Needle then was the highest structure in the city, tallest west of the Mississippi in fact. Such heights were dizzying, the kind of thing experienced by fliers, parachutists, and mountain climbers.

The top of the Needle wasn't finished yet; the floor of the restaurant level wasn't even complete. The place was swarming with workers, rushing toward their April deadline to have the tower up and running for the opening of the fair. Jeff wanted to look over the precipice, so Howard Wright let him crawl over to the rim. No rope, no harness, no net. Just like the ironworkers. He held him by the ankles as the child peered down at the city below.

Jeff Wright remembers being scared and exhilarated, but also grounded by his father's powerful hands. It was a kind of baptism in the air, where he was dipped in the heights

Opposite Page
Jeff Wright's father, Howard S. Wright, let him crawl to the edge of the unfinished Needle platform while he held his four-year-old son's legs. Wright has never forgotten the view.

and washed by the cold Pacific winds that challenged even seasoned ironworkers. He was thrilled by the new view that few had yet seen, one of the first of some 50 million visitors who have seen it since, albeit with less risk.

That view has also had an impact on many of us. While the Needle mimicked rocketry, what it still offers is a platform from which to see ourselves, gauging the scope of our region's hopes and dreams, and tracking their progress.

As the Needle went up in 1961 and became an international symbol in 1962, it was a giant yardstick. The rising tower was a kind of fundraising thermometer for World's Fair organizers, who saw ticket sales soar as the Needle did. It provided a new point of comparison for Seattle and its surroundings by making a statement about our dominant place in the region. The Needle was not only the perfect perch from which to view Mount Rainier, but also architecture's response to it, a structure that stood for the human ambitions taking shape in the city on the Sound.

It also became a way to measure ourselves against the predictions of industry, politicians, social and hard scientists, and urban planners. At the high end, it pointed to a future not unlike the fantasies of *Star Trek*; for many it promised a *Jetsons* lifestyle of futuristic ease and convenience. If the Needle's tripod has a foot in the future, it also has a foot in the present. In 1962, there was an unhindered view between the high points of the Needle and the 1914 Smith Tower, in Pioneer Square. Today, a wall of skyscrapers intervenes, evidence of a half-century of a city dramatically transformed.

Before the Needle, Seattle was mostly a low-rise city, with few new major downtown office buildings erected since the Great Depression. This photograph, taken in 1929, captures that city well. By 1961, the nearly half-century-old Smith Tower (the white tower with the pyramidal top, built in 1914) was still the tallest building in town, until the Needle topped it.

The Needle's third foot is set in the past. This symbol of the future is now historic. The occasion of its 50th anniversary is a great time to take stock of the Space Needle, to tell of its origins, to describe its highs and lows, to explore how it has changed us and the way we see ourselves. And how the world sees us. It is also a time to celebrate the vision and enthusiasm of the people who made the Needle what it is today.

A couple of months after young Jeff Wright's first precarious trip up, hundreds of people stood in line at Seattle's Olympic Hotel to apply for jobs at the Needle's restaurant-to-be. Reporter Bob Lane of the *Seattle Times* described these hopefuls as folks "with their feet on the ground and their hearts in the sky." That's the spirit that has kept the Needle turning from the day it was conceived.

The Needle's enduring presence also symbolizes a turning point in the history of our city. It is a marker of the moment when modern Seattle was born. It wouldn't be too much to claim that just as the Needle's restaurant rotates to give us a 360-degree view of the city, life in the region also revolves around it. It is a totem that tells a remarkable story.

The fair was meant to spur investor confidence in Seattle's future. In the 50 years since the fair, downtown has sprouted a high-rise skyline. In 1962, Needle visitors had an unobstructed view of the Smith Tower. Today, it's barely visible in a forest of skyscrapers.

World's Fair
Seattle, Washington 1962

CHAPTER 1

Where Do Space Needles Come From?

"We grabbed a chunk of sky and held on."

— Joseph E. Gandy, president, Century 21

In the spring of 1961, an extremely unlikely plan had started to come together, a thing that Joseph Gandy, lawyer, Ford dealer, civic leader, and former Seafair King Neptune, had called "a chunk of sky." It was the elusive and unlikely dream of Seattle hosting a modern world's fair. The respected Gandy had been appointed president of the effort. Jay Rockey, the fair's head PR man, said Gandy "knew how to make a car sale, but he was a statesman." He had taken those skills around the world to make it happen. The fair was now starting its final countdown to opening on April 21, 1962.

The fair had been nearly a decade in conception. As early as 1950, there was talk in local Chamber of Commerce circles about hosting a fair in the region. The idea had been jump-started by a small group in Seattle, led by city councilman Al Rochester. The circle expanded to include people who began to push the fair concept as a way to finally build a long-desired Civic Center in Seattle. In 1955 the state legislature in Olympia created and

Above, fair president Joseph Gandy and his wife, Laurene (second couple from left), escorted Walt Disney and his family around the fair. Disney was impressed, and predicted that Needles would soon be "cropping up" everywhere.

Opposite Page
The curved lines of the Space Needle and the Monorail helped convey the swoop and swoosh of the future: speed, height, and a new galaxy of shapes awaited us at Century 21.

The Century 21 Exposition was intended in part as a 50th-anniversary celebration of the city's first major fair, the Alaska-Yukon-Pacific Exposition of 1909. The old fairgrounds became the basis for the University of Washington campus, showing that such fairs need not be entirely ephemeral.

AYP also previewed elements that would be key to the '62 fair's success: airship flights offered Needlelike views and demonstrated that man had a future in the air.

funded a World's Fair Commission to look at the possibility of such an event. In 1956, Seattle voters approved $7.5 million to construct their Civic Center. Heading the fair commission was an energetic up-and-coming hotel executive, Edward "Eddie" Carlson, who was later to enter Seattle legend for a doodle that helped remake the city's skyline.

It began small. The original idea was to have a fair in 1959 to commemorate the 50th anniversary of Seattle's first one, the 1909 Alaska-Yukon-Pacific Exposition. In the same time period, Oregon and British Columbia would also be holding fairs or festivals to mark major anniversaries. Seattle's would be broader, with a "Festival of the West" theme, perhaps also showcasing the region's relationship with the "Orient." The scale, scope, and location were up in the air, and there was little grassroots enthusiasm to begin with. By 1958, fed up with the slow process and lack of widespread support among local leaders, *The Argus*, a downtown weekly that catered to the business community, declared the fair doomed and announced in a front-page editorial, "Let's forget the fair."

Still, a small group of business leaders continued to work on the concept. Something truly lasting and significant could be done by leveraging the Civic Center bond money into a bigger, more ambitious play that could attract state, regional, and even federal funding. Seattle could get a cluster of major facilities—a new opera house, a stadium for major

The public's first peek at the Boeing 707 prototype, the Dash 80, in 1954 was another milestone that would help make the case for a fair in Seattle. The Northwest's "Jet City" was positioned as global, forward looking, and—literally—upwardly mobile.

league sports, new theaters, perhaps even an aquarium, conservatory, or science center. The fair would be a means to a bigger end. Instead of being the usual ephemeral event, it would leave a lasting, tangible legacy. It would be, said Gandy, speaking like a car salesman, "the first truly convertible fair in history" as pavilions were adapted into permanent facilities. Some touted the possibilities of having a civic amusement zone like Copenhagen's Tivoli Gardens. Gandy compared the end result to New York's Lincoln Center.

The fair could also heighten Seattle's profile and reaffirm its clout as the Northwest's premier metropolis. Already Seattle had boosted America into the Jet Age with the Boeing 707, but a world's fair could lift the city's international standing, spur Northwest tourism, showcase Puget Sound as the future site for modern manufacturing, and raise the bar for culture.

Familiar 20th-century fair symbols were Trylon and Perisphere, the spire and globe of the 1939-40 New York World's Fair, themed "The World of Tomorrow." A temporary structure, it was torn down after the fair.

Seattle was looking to become more cosmopolitan. The old joke about the difference between San Francisco and Seattle was that "San Francisco is the mistress but Seattle is the wife." You had fun in San Francisco, but came home to Seattle to raise the kids and settle down. But Seattle wanted a little more of San Francisco's glamour if not its sin, and was looking to refine its tastes. Culture was a measure and, increasingly, so was food. From the 1950s to the 1960s, Seattle worked hard to improve its restaurant scene: more international cuisines, better chefs, dining with a view, fresh local foods. More and more restaurants began to spring up on Elliott Bay and Lake Union. Longshoremen and boatbuilders were being replaced by waitresses and wine stewards. A fair could showcase international cuisines and local foods.

Seattle too wanted more recognition for its local talent in arts and architecture. *Life* magazine had told the country about the Northwest School of art, painters such as Mark Tobey and Morris Graves. And increasingly, that creativity was showing up in distinctive architecture, a meld of Asian, Native American, modern, and mystic influences with homegrown materials that was helping to pull Seattle out of what symphony conductor Sir Thomas Beecham had once characterized as its reputation as an "aesthetic dustbin" and to burnish its reputation as a mid-century modern melting pot distinctive from any other. The fair and ensuing Civic Center could be a catalyst for the arts.

The Golden Gate Expo's centerpiece was a 400-foot-tall illuminated "needle" named the Tower of the Sun.

Also in 1939-40, San Francisco held the Golden Gate International Exposition on man-made Treasure Island in San Francisco Bay, which featured contemplative reflecting pools, arches, and gardens.

A 1950s concept drawing for a Space Age attraction at Disneyland: the TWA Moonliner rocket ride at Tomorrowland.

That it would be, could be, a true world's fair was audacious, almost preposterous. World's fairs had occurred with frequency in the United States from the mid 19th to the early 20th century, at a rate of almost one per year. But they had come to an abrupt halt with the advent of World War II, and the last U.S. fairs had been money-losers. The most recent and best-known had occurred in major cities such as New York, San Francisco, and Chicago. Now, New York and Chicago were again talking about hosting fairs. But weren't fairs over? The rise of Disneyland in Anaheim led some experts to think so. In 1957, a Stanford Research Institute report commissioned by Seattle's fair organizers contained a warning. "Extravaganzas are commonplace" was one observation. Some veterans of the last U.S. fairs, in New York and San Francisco (1939-40), believed that "the day of the 'old fashioned world's fair' is past." To host a fair, Seattle would have to reinvent the medium. "If the Seattle fair is a flop . . . fairs will have had it," predicted Gandy.

After a hiatus of more than 20 years, how likely was it that the rebirth of U.S. world's fairs would occur in a provincial, second-tier city? Seattle was the 19th-largest city in America in 1960, with a population of 557,087, just ahead of Buffalo, Cincinnati, and Memphis. Could a city that size draw the 7 to 10 million visitors it would take to make the fair a success? Washington State's total population was only 2.8 million, and the entire combined population of the region, adding in Oregon, British Columbia, and Alaska, was still only 6.5 million. Seattle was tucked into the far northwest corner of the lower 48 and previously known as the Gateway to Alaska. *Newsweek* magazine wrote that prior to Century 21, the biggest regional event had been "the arrival of Lewis and Clark."

Overseas, Seattle was a nonentity. When Joe Gandy went abroad to sell the fair, in some cases he had to use custom-made maps to show prospects where Seattle was, and teach them how to pronounce its name.

As time went on, the fair organizers began to reshape their ideas opportunistically. After the Soviets launched *Sputnik* and eyes turned skyward, Washington Senator Warren G. Magnuson told fair boosters that he could help them get federal money if they shifted focus to a science-themed exposition. Thus was the idea of Century 21 born, a future-oriented fair devoted to the Space Age. Seattle received an initial federal commitment of $9 million for a science pavilion with the backing of President Dwight Eisenhower, and the fair came to life during the New Frontier and new presidency of John F. Kennedy.

The fair now had a raison d'etre—it was part of a national mission. It also had a unique angle: no previous fair had been so focused on science, and this science came with the excitement of space exploration. Seattle was poised to seize the *Sputnik* moment.

And Gandy's persistence had paid off. He had traveled to Paris to put the fair plans before the Bureau of International Expositions, the BIE, the international treaty organization that sanctioned world's fairs. Faced with competition from the planners of New York's proposed 1964-65 fair, with the Seattle fair already delayed from its original target date of 1959, he'd also had to agree to follow BIE rules that required Seattle to limit its fair to a single six-month season instead of two, making it much more difficult, as conventional wisdom had it, to generate a profit. But Seattle needed BIE sanction because of the status it conferred and doors it opened. It was, as Gandy put it, his "hunting license" for international involvement. With it, he could talk to foreign governments about exhibiting in Seattle. Major international representation would be impossible without BIE approval, and without it, who was going to take a festival in far-flung Seattle seriously?

Seattle got the BIE's okay, and in 1960 the diplomat-salesman Gandy was off to round up exhibitors. In Seattle the fair organizers, with millions of taxpayer funds at hand, were raising additional millions in private investment to get things moving. Bulldozers had begun clearing the Warren Avenue neighborhood at the foot of Queen Anne Hill, which was selected as the site of the new fair and Civic Center because there was so much reusable infrastructure already in place: the Ice Arena, the old Armory, Civic Auditorium, Memorial

The Eiffel Tower in Paris is the granddaddy of world's fair legacy structures. Built for the Paris Exposition Universelle in 1889—the same year as the Great Seattle Fire—the tower has become an example of both the ingenuity and the legacy that fairs can produce. It is also an international symbol of the city itself and directly inspired Seattle's ambitious Needle-builders.

Stadium, utilities, a street grid. Seattle organizers cleared out the rest of the neighborhood on a 74-acre campus. Instead of a large fair site on undeveloped property that might become a park, Seattle's would be compact, tucked into the central city between the waterfront on the west and a major highway (99) on the east, between a residential neighborhood to the north and the commercial district to the south. It would be dense with features that would benefit the city for the long term.

The site would partly fulfill the promise of the Denny Regrade, a turn-of-the-century project that leveled the land in what is now Belltown for the city's expansion. An earlier scheme to remake Seattle had been proposed for the area, including a government civic center, but voters had turned down the so-called Bogue Plan in 1912. The new Civic Center, different in location and more cultural in character than Bogue's concept, was based on the vision of extending the urban core and linking the new cultural nexus to downtown with a mass transit component, which became the Monorail.

One of the Northwest's great modern architects, Paul Thiry, had been appointed as chief architect of the fair in 1958, and was responsible for herding architectural cats that included much of the region's best talent, plus outside advisers of national repute. His challenge was to create a coherent, cutting-edge fair that could display new building materials and techniques, and also segue neatly into the everyday Civic Center that would remain after the exposition.

One drawback of the chosen site was that it was low, at the base of one of Seattle's tallest hills, Queen Anne (456 feet). Much of the area had been flat and open between Puget Sound and Lake Union, used by Native Americans for hunting and for crossing between the two bodies of water. Later it had become the farm of one of the city's founding families, the Dennys. It was suitable for building, peppered with "keeper" structures, but one thing was missing: a view.

And that was a problem. Organizers had considered numerous locations for both the Civic Center and the fair. First Hill (near Harborview Hospital), Fort Lawton (now Discovery Park), Sand Point Naval Air Station (now Magnuson Park), and Duwamish Head were among those proposed and discussed. A common virtue was that they showcased the natural beauty surrounding Seattle: Puget Sound, the lakes, the Olympics and Cascades. These were nature's impressive pavilions. The AYP Exposition in '09, laid out by the Olmsteds, had prominently featured a view corridor that framed Mount Rainier, a postcard vista still extant at the University of Washington campus on a clear day. Fair organizers knew that capitalizing on the scenery was essential to showcasing the city's stunning setting, but how?

The Seattle fair organizers chose architect Paul Thiry, often called the "father of Northwest modernism," to oversee the planning and architecture of the fair site. Thiry had been inspired by previous world's fairs and studied them in preparation for Seattle's.

The site for the Needle was unglamorous, but the tower would do what the lay of the land would not: provide a spectacular view of the surrounding region.

London's Crystal Palace was the defining monument of the very first world's fair, held in 1851, the same year that Seattle's founders raised the first log cabin on Alki Point. The Palace set the standard for expo architecture being grand and innovative.

Another problem loomed: As Thiry and others worked on plans for the site, no structure yet stood out as the kind of landmark that fairs so often create, either as a symbol to promote the fair itself or as a permanent legacy. Viewing platforms, sky rides, bell towers—these were common architectural highlights at major expositions.

London's Crystal Palace Exhibition of 1851, the very first world's fair, was named for its wonder, an innovative iron-and-glass building that contained marvelous exhibits. Nothing had so captured the imagination of the Victorian age as the glittering dome, beneath which were displayed the works of all "civilized" nations. The year the Crystal Palace opened in Hyde Park, advance scouts for the Denny Party were also building something historic here: Seattle's first log cabin. Seattle was founded in the year the modern world's fair was invented.

In 1853, at America's first international exposition, New York organizers had also built their own knockoff of the Crystal Palace. More interesting, though, was a tower constructed as a private venture right next door. Called Latting Observatory, it was a 315-foot-high tapered wood-and-iron structure that was the tallest in New York. You could ride a steam-powered elevator to the top and with telescopes see as far as New Jersey. A teenaged fairgoer named Samuel Clemens dubbed the view "grand."

Chicago in 1893 had its magnificently enormous steel contraption, the Ferris Wheel, which served as a kind of moving high-rise landmark for the World's Columbian Exposition and popularized a ride familiar, usually on a smaller scale, in every amusement park. The vast Chicago wheel carried passengers in cars the size of Metro buses, and became one of the most popular attractions of the fair.

The New York fair of 1939-40 had made the globe-and-pyramid Trylon and Perisphere among the most familiar objects in newsreels of the '30s, though they were demolished after the fair.

The most recent world's fair, in Brussels in 1958, had featured an innovative modernist structure called the Atomium, based on a billions-times magnification of a carbon crystal. Looking like a molecular model made from metallic Tinker Toys, it featured view platforms and a restaurant. It was emblematic of the new postwar atomic era.

The ultimate exposition legacy was the Eiffel Tower, built for the Paris Exposition Universelle of 1889, the year when the commercial district of a young, bustling port city named Seattle

Chicago's impressive Ferris Wheel in 1893 gave fairgoers a view and proved that a fair's symbolic structure could also offer a memorable ride.

burned to the ground. The Eiffel Tower had come to symbolize the City of Light, an instantly recognizable monument that offered views and fine French food, and showcased the innovations of turn-of-the-century architecture and engineering. It had also become a symbol of expositions themselves, with their power to remake and rebrand a city, to embody an age to come, and yet be somehow ageless. In 1961, as now, the Eiffel Tower was as unique, modern, and cosmopolitan as it was when it was built, maybe more so. Much imitated, it still stood unmatched. It had become not only an icon, but an icon of icons.

If Seattle was going to host a world's fair, it would have to create a landmark symbol that could broadcast its messages to the world. Ideally, it would be more than a one-off wonder, both inspirational and as permanent as the Civic Center itself.

Could Seattle grab an even bigger chunk of sky? Could it build an Eiffel Tower fit for the Space Age?

The American Space Age really began with the launch of the first U.S. astronaut, Alan Shepard, into space on May 5, 1961, in the *Freedom 7* capsule. In that same month, the Space Needle's foundation was poured and the symbol of the era began its fast rise in Seattle.

CHAPTER 2

Sleepless in Stuttgart, Obsessed in Seattle

"It's in the wind."

— Paul Thiry, Century 21 architect

It's nice to believe that, like most brilliant breakthroughs, the Space Needle came together in a single "eureka" moment, and the story of its origins is often told that way.

The tale usually begins with a trip to Germany in April 1959 by Western International Hotels executive Eddie Carlson, the man who was to volunteer his time for eight years and was almost single-handedly responsible for the Seattle World's Fair getting off the ground.

Carlson was chair of the state fair commission; he also preceded Joe Gandy as first president of Century 21, the group that organized and ran the fair, and was Century 21's chairman. He played a major role in the development of Seattle Center too, heading up the conversion of the U.S. Science Pavilion into the permanent Pacific Science Center when the fair closed. He also acted as host of legendary 7 a.m. breakfast meetings at one of Western's hotels, The Olympic, where fair organizers met before the workday to plot, strategize, and problem solve.

But Carlson also played a pivotal role in the creation and operation of the Space Needle. He knew that the fair needed an icon, something to boost its "wow" factor. While on a trip to Europe, Carlson and his wife, Nell, and their friends Webb and Virginia Moffett stopped in Stuttgart, Germany, to pick up a new Mercedes (a white 190SL) the Moffetts would be using for their tour of the continent. The car wasn't ready, so they had a free night in town. On a friend's recommendation they had dinner at a restaurant built like a crow's nest atop a 711-foot-high broadcast tower. The view was great from the observation platform, and the dining room was crowded on a weeknight. Being in the hospitality business, Carlson was impressed.

After a restless night, suffering from jet lag and being unable to let go of the cares of the fair at the start of his vacation, Carlson got up early the next morning. Alone in the coffee shop of the Graf Zeppelin Hotel, he sketched something resembling a ring or a flying saucer at the top of an obelisk, and wrote the words "Space Needle" under it.* "Space" was

*An interesting unresolved bit of history is just what Eddie Carlson drew his doodle on: a placemat, napkin, or something else? In Carlson's 1989 memoir, *Recollections of a Lucky Fellow*, he remembered it was a placemat. That's what Murray Morgan wrote in his official 1963 history of the fair, *Century 21*. That should settle it. However, Carlson himself also referred to it as a napkin in a 1981 *Seattle Times* interview, and napkin references gained currency after a 1987 KCTS-TV interview with Walt Crowley in which Carlson redrew the Needle sketch on a cocktail napkin. Most accounts suggest that Carlson also sent a doodle from Stuttgart to Seattle on a postcard. Neither the original placemat, napkin, nor postcard has ever turned up.

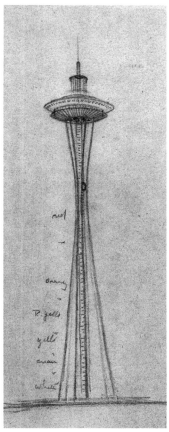

On the drawing board, the Needle went through many versions as its designers refined the concept. These drawings from John Graham & Co. show refinements and reworking of the top house to get its final shape (left) and even sketch an idea (above) to give the tower a rainbow-type color scheme, starting with white on the bottom and ranging to red at the top.

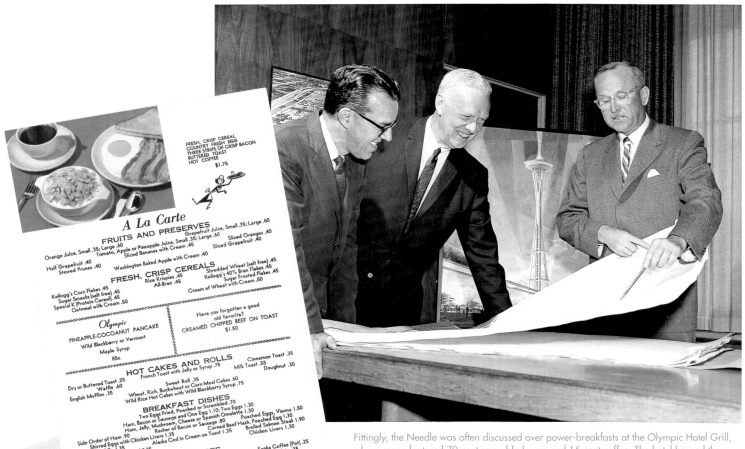

Fittingly, the Needle was often discussed over power-breakfasts at the Olympic Hotel Grill, whose menu featured 70-cent scrambled eggs and 15-cent coffee. The hotel housed the office of hotel executive and fair organizer Eddie Carlson, seen above (on the left) going over Needle plans with Jim Douglas and architect John Graham Jr., who helped him bring the Stuttgart doodle to reality.

the emerging theme of the fair, and "needle" is a term for tall pillars and also the pointer on a compass. A skyward-pointing needle was potent symbolism for Space Age America. "It occurred to me," Carlson later reflected, "that if we could build a similar tower in Seattle, it could serve as a symbol not only for the period of the fair, but like the Eiffel Tower and the Empire State Building, it could become a permanent, easily recognizable symbol of its locality."

Carlson gathered every bit of information that he could. Towers, he thought, made an impression in cities like Paris, New York, Tokyo, even Pisa. After Carlson visited the Eiffel Tower on the same trip, the Space Needle "became an obsession," he said.

When he returned home, Carlson sought out his friend Jim Douglas to act as a sounding board. Douglas was vice president of Century 21 and president of the Northgate shopping center. Carlson thought Douglas would hear out his tower scheme without rejecting it before he was through. He "would not immediately say, 'That has to be the craziest idea I've ever heard,'" Carlson remembered.

A visit to the Stuttgart Tower proved a revelation for Carlson. Here was a broadcast mast that also offered incredible views and featured restaurants that were crowded even on weeknights. That suggested a business model for something that would outlast a fair.

The Empire State Building was studied by the Needle builders as a skyline structure that offered an observation deck visited by millions.

After hearing about Carlson's idea, Douglas suggested they talk to architect John "Jack" Graham Jr., who like his father, John Graham Sr., had helped to reshape Seattle with major projects. Jack Graham had branched out to emerging suburban landscapes too. One of his claims to fame was designing the first successful car-oriented mall in America, Northgate in north Seattle, a profitable model that was copied the world over.

Architect John Graham was already working on a rotating restaurant at the Ala Moana shopping center in Honolulu, Hawaii, when Carlson brought him the idea for the Needle. It too had the profile of a flying saucer.

A possible Needle influence was Buckminster Fuller's Dymaxion House, a circular home with windows all around. A surviving prototype is in the Henry Ford Museum.

Carlson and Douglas met with Graham and pitched him on the Needle. Graham agreed to speculate by providing design work while leaving it to Carlson and Douglas to figure out the financing.

It so happened that Graham's firm was working on a revolving, saucer-shaped restaurant, La Ronde, for the top of an office building at the Ala Moana shopping center in Honolulu, Hawaii (La Ronde opened in November 1961). Could that idea be adapted for the Needle? Graham thought it could. He knew how to build successful commercial structures, and he eventually patented a mechanism that enabled a dining-room turntable to turn. Graham had also studied at Yale and had there been exposed to Buckminster Fuller's Dymaxion House, which featured a circular home around a central mast with a pointy top and windows all around. A rotating tower restaurant that capitalized on the city's scenery was a compelling concept, one that added a new twist to the Stuttgart version.

Paul Thiry later said that Graham had a knack for seeing ahead, like figuring out the impact of the expanding highway system on shopping patterns. "He was kind of clairvoyant," Thiry remarked.

Thiry, the fair's head architect, was no stranger to the future himself. He had visited and studied numerous world's fairs, and had been heavily influenced as a young architect when he visited Chicago's Century of Progress Exposition (1933-34). It was a Deco-Moderne dream world with many innovative architectural techniques on display. "It was extraordinary," Thiry remembered. "It was a museum of new architectural styles and construction techniques, of city plans and new technologies."

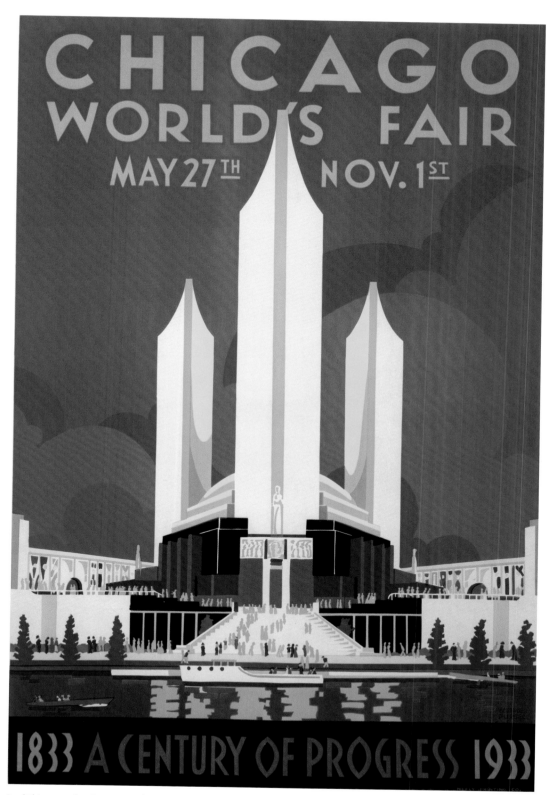

Paul Thiry was deeply impressed with Chicago's Century of Progress Exposition of 1933-34, a showcase of futuristic design.

Thiry not only planned the fair site, he also designed some of its major pavilions, including the Coliseum and the Ford Motor Co. Pavilion, shown in his sketch above with the Needle looming behind it.

Thiry wanted the fair to be a showcase of modern design and Northwest talent. One of the impressive legacy structures was the U.S. Science Pavilion (now Pacific Science Center). Gathered around the model are Yamasaki assistant William Ku, Perry B. Johanson of Seattle's NBBJ architects, Philip Evans of the U.S. Science Exhibit, Francis D. Miller, Deputy Commissioner of the exhibit, and its architect, Minoru Yamasaki.

As master of the Seattle fair site, Thiry had been looking for a landmark structure. He was himself designing the Century 21 Coliseum, a vast concrete structure (known today as Key Arena). He viewed it as a "workhorse" structure designed to house many events and exhibits and have a flexible interior that could be easily rearranged in multiple configurations. The squat pyramid was an impressive anchor for the fair site, but it didn't pass muster as a compelling symbol of the exposition's reach-for-the-stars theme.

Thiry also wanted to "bring the fair to the Sound." He and other fair planners brainstormed schemes to link the fair to the waterfront. A skyride and ramps to the Elliott Bay piers to ease visitation by cruise ship passengers were considered. Another idea floated was connecting the grounds to the Sound with a salmon stream.

Yet another was to design a raised pavilion to give people a view of the Sound and the Olympics. Before the Needle, there was Thiry's concept for what became the U.S. Science Pavilion: a raised 20-sided structure of pentagonal panels called the Cosmodrome that would connect man with his "emergence from the primeval sea." Preliminary drawings of the fair show the Cosmodrome as a signature pre-Needle structure rising above a large man-made lagoon.

The actual U.S. Science Pavilion, designed by architect Minoru Yamasaki, turned out very different. Thiry had little control because Yamasaki had the full confidence and funding of the federal government to do as he liked on the site, which is at the high point of the 74-acre campus. Thiry urged him to take advantage of the location and lift the structure so visitors to the pavilion could get a scenic view. Yamasaki instead chose to build close to the ground. The pavilion's courtyard featured pools and fountains, but it was a closed campus within the fair's already enclosed site, a compound within a compound. "There were some advocates of a solid, high building with a view. . . . We wanted to create a place of serenity," Yamasaki later explained.

Almost everyone loved the result, however, inspired by Yamasaki's "Space Gothic" arches rising above an oasis of sparkling purity. *Time* magazine called it a "modern Xanadu." But it did not fulfill the role of either being an icon or showing off Seattle's spectacular setting. The Eiffel Tower it most definitely wasn't.

The idea of a Seattle tower for the fair did not originate with Carlson, though his trip to Stuttgart and revelation there proved to be a catalyst. As Thiry was casting around for a structure that would do the job, others were sketching ideas and pitching concepts. The Eiffel Tower was of course a model. Also, tall radio towers and more recent TV towers, such as the ones newly placed on top of Queen Anne Hill.

In 1959, the Japanese built the 1,092-foot Tokyo TV Tower, which looked like a replica of the Eiffel Tower. In the mid-1950s, Europeans began experimenting with tall, tapered concrete towers with needlelike broadcast masts on top. The Stuttgart Tower, built in 1956, was one of these. Taking a cue from Stuttgart was not Carlson's idea alone.

In fact, the idea had been pitched in *The Argus*, a weekly newspaper that amounted to Seattle's version of the *Wall Street Journal*. On February 28, 1958, more than a year before Carlson visited Stuttgart, a story ran under the headline: "A World Fair Landmark: Build a Single TV Tower-Restaurant at Civic Center-World Fair?" It was written by a Seattle freelance writer, Erna Kalland, who proposed that a monument based on the Stuttgart Tower be built for the fair. A drawing of it ran with the story, showing the tower's restaurant and needlelike profile.

Kalland had recently visited Stuttgart, where she'd had her own Eddie Carlson moment as a guest of South German Broadcasting. In her article, she described the two elevators that whisked guests up and down the shaft of the Stuttgart Tower to one of two restaurants (one featuring casual dining, the other gourmet cuisine) and an observation platform above them both. "When (and not if) Washington State has its International Exposition in Seattle in 1961-62, there should be a symbol marking her dramatically as the Northwest cornerstone of the United States, a symbol which draws people from afar and defies the imagination. Why not choose a tower, as Mr. Eiffel did for the Paris Exposition?" Kalland argued. "From the top of such a tower every point of its 360-degree view would give the viewer an unforgettable panorama. It is just one step from the idea of such an observation platform to that of a restaurant too."

THE TWO SENTRIES, THE 42 STORY L. C. SMITH BUILDING AND

MT. RAINIER, SEATTLE, U. S. A.

Before the Needle, the Smith Tower, finished in 1914, was the tallest building in Seattle. Its white color and pyramidal top seemed to complement the snowy cone and color scheme of Mount Rainier.

She also quoted Paul Thiry at length supporting the concept: "'Our Planning Commission definitely should exploit such an engineering feat,' continues Mr. Thiry, who is a member of this group as well as the Design Standards Advisory Board [of the world's fair]. 'The design should be chosen on a competitive basis and the tower built by private enterprise.'"

Kalland concluded: "Nature presented us with Mt. Rainier and a magnificent though idle harbor; human ingenuity created the Boeing airplane factory. Now we need an imaginative and yet practical symbol for the 1961 International Exposition."

At the same time there was a movement afoot to persuade fair planners to move the fair south to a site between Seattle and Tacoma. An Army depot in Auburn was suggested, and on June 22, 1958, the *Tacoma News Tribune* published a front-page picture of a needle-like tower with a tall shaft and a flying-saucer top. This was combined with a monorail concept. Rocketlike gondola cars on wire would move visitors around the fairgrounds, then climb a tall coil to the top of the tower, "to a dining room hundreds of feet off the ground . . . tying in with the Space Age." The tower was conceived by a man named Bert Smyser, who had designed Washington State exhibits for the 1939-40 world's fairs in San Francisco and New York. He designed one other famous local landmark: Tacoma's Java Jive coffee pot building.

This view of Seattle and Mount Rainier was shot from Queen Anne Hill before the Needle was built.

In 1962, the newly completed Needle inspired a rash of skyline photographs showing how the contemporary city compared with the old one, and the great mountain beyond.

In 1932, the prominent industrial designer Norman Bel Geddes published his concept for a tower with rotating partial disks housing restaurants and observation platforms for the 1933-34 Chicago world's fair. It was never built.

The famous modern industrial designer Norman Bel Geddes had proposed a tower for the 1933-34 Chicago fair that featured a straight, three-sided shaft with three cantilevered partial disks that rotated in a circle nearly 300 feet in the air. The disks were designed to house three revolving restaurants for patrons who would be taken up in elevators. Bel Geddes wrote, "I see no reason why architecture should not be utilized as an added attraction for the restaurant, if it can be interesting and so join in the spirit of the occasion." It was never built, but the concept was published in Bel Geddes's 1932 book, *Horizons*. It was similar enough that a lawyer for Bel Geddes's widow (the designer had died in 1958) wrote to Eddie Carlson in February 1962, pointing out the similarity in design and asking for an explanation. Harry Henke III, assistant vice president of Century 21, forwarded the complaint to Needle president Bagley Wright, wryly writing, "My only comment is that in the event you have to take it down, I wish you would wait until after the fair is over."

Years later, Thiry described the architectural context in which the Seattle tower concept emerged. He cited the influence of the Stuttgart Tower, and a mid-1950s proposal of a needlelike Freedom Tower for a proposed permanent exposition called Interama in Miami, Florida. "The idea [for the Needle], it's original to a point, but . . . it's part of the wind. It's in the wind," he said. At mid-century, such ideas were wafting through many imaginations.

Jack Graham's crew now had the challenge of catching the wind and pulling together a concrete plan for a permanent landmark in the sky that could be up and running in 1962. It would have to serve symbolic and practical purposes, delight the public, and have a viable, sustainable business model for the long-term future. That would take considerable "human ingenuity" indeed.

As historian Murray Morgan related in his book on the fair, *Century 21: The Story of the Seattle World's Fair, 1962*, the Needle concept got more complicated before it got less. Jack Graham put his team on it before the Needle was a paying client. They began to explore different concepts, different mixes of uses. Some of the early fair concepts involved water (Thiry's "primeval sea," possibly an aquarium), a rotating restaurant, an observation deck, a TV tower, a heliport, perhaps even a sky-high planetarium. A congressman from New York, Victor Anfuso, suggested that a "high directional radar antenna" be installed on top of the tower for "the purpose of bouncing signals off the Moon." The creative ideas flowed, and what became the Needle first gained a lot of conceptual baggage before slimming down to its final form. But there were also major practical questions unanswered. What would it cost, who would pay for it, what would it be made of, where would it go, and what would keep it going after the fair?

These were big questions, and time was running short.

Opposite Page
An early concept showed how a tower would fit into an imagined fairground setting. A number of early concepts sought to connect the fair and its pavilions with water features and aquatic themes.

CHAPTER 3

The Coming of the Saucer

"You have to make the top house flatter, more like a flying saucer, like this—more disky."
— John Graham Jr., Space Needle architect

The general public first saw the John Graham & Co. concept for the Space Needle on September 12, 1960, when it appeared on the front page of the *Seattle Times*. The Needle was in the form of a sleek 500- to 550-foot tapered tower with a flying saucer resting on top. Far from a final plan, this was an already out-of-date rendering of the Needle design. The tower shown in the paper was made of concrete, but it would later become steel. Its straight vertical shaft would evolve into a tripod with a sheaf shape, wide at the bottom, thinning to a narrow waist on high, then widening out again with six long arms holding a round top house, like a waitress balancing a serving tray on fingertips.

Much would change between the fall debut and the actual Needle that opened in the spring of 1962, but basic elements were in place: a restaurant turning at the speed of one revolution per hour, topped by an observation deck giving visitors a 360-degree view of the countryside, both reached by capsulelike elevators. And the futuristic look: the drawing of the Needle resembled the landmark we know today, but without the finesse or grace of the finished product. Some earlier designs looked like a bagel on a spike, or a tethered balloon captured in a net, even a cocktail shaker. But now the Needle was beginning to take on a more interesting, even inspiring form.

The Needle also came with big questions, and one of them was right there in the *Times* headline: "Who'll Finance?" As the project went public, it was uncertain who would pay for it. The feds, state, and city had already invested heavily in the fair. Would the late-arriving Needle be built with public funds or paid for by private investors? Its exact location on the fair site was still unknown. A proposed site plan for the fair by architect Paul Thiry showed the "Space Needle" added in by hand in August 1960, located between the Science Pavilion and the Armory, about where the Paul Horiuchi Mural Amphitheatre is today. It was a major piece of the fair puzzle and would have to be fit in somewhere on the crowded fairgrounds.

The early cost estimate was $2-2.5 million, a lot of money. There was no zoning for such a project, no final plan—only very preliminary engineering—no city permits, no approvals. "I expect this to get built," Century 21's ever-optimistic president, Joe Gandy, told the paper. But first, "this" had to evolve some more, and many questions had to be answered.

Opposite Page
In September 1960, the public got its first look at the Needle concept, presented here by Barbara Bye of the Century 21 staff. This version of the tower featured a saucer on top of a concrete cruciform shaft. The final tripod concept was in the works, but not yet unveiled.

To get the Needle built would take a huge team effort among designers, builders, investors, business leaders, and public officials. The fair organizers put on a full-court press, expressed in their body language. Standing, from left, are Fred Paulsell, Edward Tremper, Robert Colwell, Otto Brandt, and Lee Moran. Seated, from left, are Jim Douglas, Iver Cederwall, Sen. Warren G. Magnuson, and Eddie Carlson.

John Graham & Co. was known for being a businessman's architectural firm, a full-service, pragmatic, get-it-done-on-time-and-on-budget concern. But the firm was not without imagination. According to Eddie Carlson, it was one of the city's major firms still without a world's fair commission, though its architects had been working on some big concepts, including Jim Jackson's idea for an aquarium that visitors could walk underneath in a transparent tunnel while watching the fish swimming overhead.

Still, when Graham described his goals for the Space Needle on the eve of the opening of the World's Fair, he broke it down efficiently and prosaically in executive fashion: "The Space Needle was designed to satisfy three objectives: To symbolize 'Man in the Space Age,' to provide 'gate appeal' and to produce a permanent profit-making attraction."

The first two sounded easy, but they were not. How do you embody a New Frontier that human beings are just beginning to explore? Sputnik and even the early Gemini space capsules were little more than tin cans shot into orbit. Glamorous as the "Right Stuff" astronauts and the early launches were, the world of the 21st century had to promise more. It had to straddle science fact and science fiction. But it couldn't look old school: Buck Rogers and Captain Video weren't going to do it.

One pre-Needle concept from John Graham & Co. for a fair legacy structure was a landed-saucer restaurant over a man-made lagoon.

Fortunately, there was inspiration close at hand. Seattle's premier natural backdrop had played a role in the most sensational space craze of the postwar period: the UFO phenomenon. On June 24, 1947, a Boise, Idaho, businessman and pilot named Kenneth Arnold, flying east between Mount Rainier and Mount Adams from Chehalis to Yakima, spotted what he described as fast-flying objects that he likened to plates or disks skipping through the sky near Rainier. His report hit the headlines, and the phenomenon of "flying saucers" was born. Soon, everyone was seeing them. On June 27, the *Times* front-page headline read, "Residents of Seattle See Mysterious Flying Disks." On July 5, the paper ran a photograph of one taken by a Coast Guard yeoman in North Seattle ("Camera Shoots Mysterious Disk Over North End"). Experts tried to explain them away, but soon a nation was gripped by unidentified flying objects.

The saucers fed both Cold War fear and the excitement about what we humans might find among the stars just as our technology was enabling us to begin reaching for them. Space Age forms were taking shape in postwar "Googie" architecture as roadside attractions featuring rockets, satellites, planets, and saucers to capture the public's attention. Arnold, who later wrote a book on UFOs called *The Coming of the Saucers*, was baffled by the phenomenon that consumed the country. "Half the people look at me as a combination of Einstein, Flash Gordon and screwball," he said. And when you think about it, that's just about the right formula for Space Age world's fair architecture. It needed to be smart, futuristic, and fun.

While UFOs came to represent crackpot paranoia or archetypal obsession (even the psychoanalyst Carl Jung wrote a book about their meaning), they also represented a sneak preview of the future, what Harvard professor David Menzel, the chief space adviser to the fair, called "space travel in reverse." UFO believers speculated that superior beings had

Among the rejected concepts for the Needle: a restaurant tower, this one by John Graham & Co. architect Art Edwards, which featured a domed planetarium on top.

developed highly advanced technology beyond our own and were observing us. Earthlings could barely shoot monkeys and dogs into orbit, yet saucers, real or imagined, could cross the solar system, even the galaxy, and whisk beings between worlds. Our government might have been getting its hands on that technology: Days after Arnold's Mount Rainier disks sighting, the local paper in Roswell, New Mexico, announced that the Air Force had captured a flying saucer. They might be piloted by snooping aliens, but wasn't that our hope too? Didn't we want to become the "aliens" exploring other planets someday?

Century 21 would feature space rides, from the Boeing Spacearium's tour of the universe to the Gayway's tacky dark ride, Flight to Mars, which became a beloved feature of the postfair Fun Forest. Menzel himself had proposed a rocket tower and giant moon replica for the fair. But the Needle would represent a saucer in captivity, "pinned," historian James Gilbert has written, "to the Seattle skyline like a mounted butterfly." A spinning saucer-shaped restaurant would offer another kind of trip: a chance to sip cocktails and contemplate Mount Rainier eye-to-eye. If one were lucky, it might be on a day when strange saucer-shaped lenticular clouds formed over Rainier's massive dome. The glacier-covered mountain had helped to shape the Puget Sound basin's landscape, but it was also the birthplace of a new Space Age mythology.

The key for Graham, with Eddie Carlson's doodle in mind, was to find some combination of tower and top that fulfilled all the goals of space, gate, and permanence. Graham personally oversaw Needle development. His staff, a team of about 10 designers, according to Graham architect Rod Kirkwood, worked on many versions and parts of the Needle concept. "It was a team effort," Graham said in 1961. They had already turned to the saucer shape for the rotating bar and restaurant they were building in Hawaii. It should work even better in the Seattle context, especially when set off on a tower of its own, the tallest structure in the region.

As the Needle opened in April 1962, Graham was more specific about its origins. The *Seattle Post-Intelligencer* reported: "Graham credits designer Arthur E. Edwards with the idea for the Space Needle, based partly on a plan evolved by John Ridley for a revolving restaurant atop a 25-story building, which Graham's firm was designing in Honolulu. 'Edwards' idea called for a revolving restaurant shaped like a flying saucer on the top of a thick monolith, higher than the Washington Monument. Everyone agreed that this concept met the three objectives. It combined a spectacular symbol with a structure that has a profit potential and lasting appeal,' Graham declared."

At one point or another, just about everyone in Graham's firm had a hand in shaping the Needle. Edwards worked on the shafted saucer; Ridley imagined a structure caged in crossed cables, cinched in the center for an hourglass shape, or later in plastic form concrete. Over time, the hourglass morphed into a tripod without cables, and the flying saucer top continued to flatten. Graham had told his architects and designers to let their imaginations fly, but he was there to direct the work through the iterations. What he sought, he told the staff, was "a tower unique and inspiring."

Another early (1959) Art Edwards concept featured a cable-tethered tower restaurant, this one resembling the shape of a cocktail shaker.

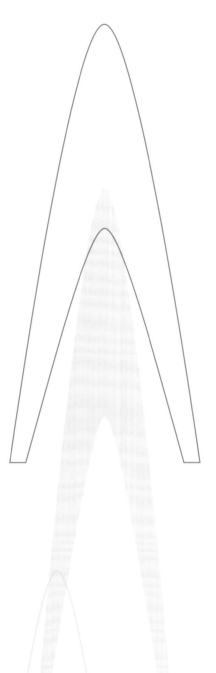

Graham architects experimented with models to test color schemes. How would red and orange look against Seattle's (rare) blue skies?

Harnessing all that talent wasn't easy. Eddie Carlson later wrote: "Jack's office moved ahead with sketches. His very talented architectural team was challenged with the design concept but was struggling with a solution that would satisfy Jack Graham's critique. At times, the Needle seemed weighed down by too many concepts. Graham pushed for something striking and simple. At one session, he said, 'You have to make the top house flatter, more like a flying saucer, like this—more disky.'" A rudimentary overlay sketch that Graham made on August 2, 1960, shows, in basic lines like Carlson's own fabled doodle, a shaft and a saucer top. That drawing came more than a year after Carlson had first brought the Needle concept to Graham, and less than two months before the in-progress Needle concept hit the papers.

In the summer of 1960, after a year at the drawing boards, Graham decided to bring in some outside help. He turned to University of Washington architecture professor Victor Steinbrueck, who was tapped for the Needle project by his friend and neighbor Nathan Wilkinson Jr., a Graham partner. Wilkinson described it as "a summer vacation assignment." Edwards, Jackson, and Ridley were mostly busy on other work that summer.

Steinbrueck was intrigued with the project, and wasn't busy with other commissions. He came on board at $5 per hour to work in the Graham office and move the Needle through the conceptual process.

Steinbrueck's focus was the tower, and he sketched many different concepts and versions— he estimated that he made 1,000 drawings or more. Over time, he homed in on a structure with a narrow waist, an approach that Graham architect Ridley had also been sketching as a tripod. Steinbrueck had become entranced by the form of a smooth wooden sculpture

Drawings of the fairgrounds often had to go out before the design was finalized. This rendering shows the final Needle tripod, but the top house is an earlier version. The image emphasizes the fair, downtown, and Mount Rainier, but the rest of the city has simply been erased.

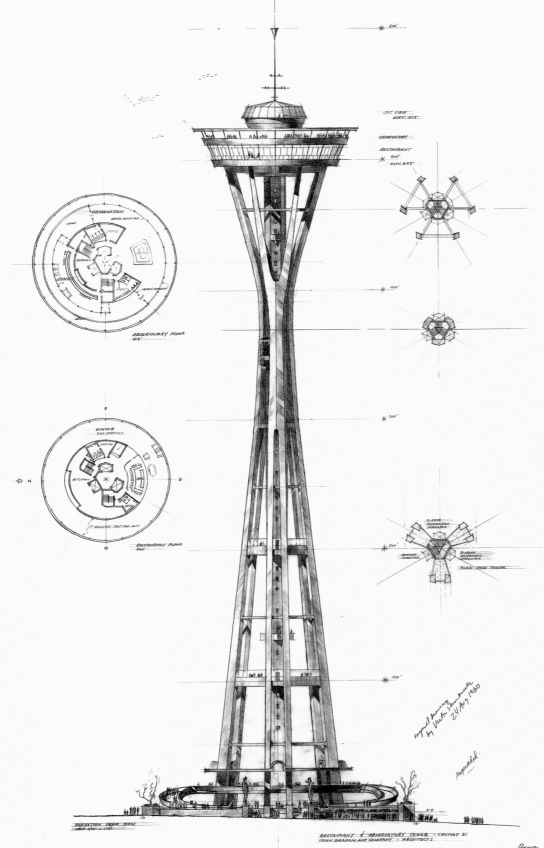

50

he owned by California modern artist David Lemon. It was an abstract figure with three legs rising to a narrow waist, then arms extending upward. Its name: "The Feminine One."

In August 1960 he made a sketch that translated the sculpture into the Needle: "In the tower form, it was conceived as three figures leaning back together against the core, which was to be minimized and separate in feeling. When I did it I realized very definitely that the price for the aesthetic or sculptural tension and consequential grace was that of making it difficult structurally. I knew I was making it hard for the engineers." He felt sure he had made a breakthrough. "I spent the weekend developing that idea and brought it to the office on Monday morning. They immediately went for it," he later wrote.

The Needle still required refinement, and the Graham team continued to work on it. The top house was also still evolving and had yet to get its distinctive pagoda top. It also had

Architect Victor Steinbrueck was hired by John Graham & Co. to work toward the final needle design as a summer project in 1960. He found inspiration for the tower tripod in a sculpture called "The Feminine One" by artist David Lemon.

Opposite Page
Steinbrueck's steel tripod and top-house refinements gave the Needle a kind of graceful swoop that had been lacking in some of the earlier designs, and the wasp waist became part of its signature look. It also made people wonder if the tower was stronger than it looked. It was.

to get bigger in order to host enough diners to make the planned restaurant profitable—an economically sustainable Space Needle was essential—but it couldn't get too big or else they would run into problems with city code. Graham insisted the top house maintain a "disky" profile. It was already five stories tall, but the distinctive flattening effect was partly achieved when Nathan Wilkinson suggested they expose the support beams, which created the "sunburst," an idea sparked by seeing exposed beams during the under-construction Ala Moana project. Ridley added the hallmark "halo" feature to the design, which also enhanced the saucer effect, and gave the top its distinctive curves. Graham also wanted elevators on the outside of the tower, understanding that they would turn a visit to the Needle into a spectacular ride. The final design had three capsules running up the inner core instead of outside on a shaft. That enhanced the drama of the ride. Even now, patrons are startled by the views, the speed, and passing so close to parts of the structure. In addition, the doors opened to the outside, which spiced up the effect. Multiple view platforms at the 100-foot and 200-foot levels were considered, and a spiral entry ramp was designed for the base.

As work progressed, there was a growing realization that a concrete tower would likely take too long and that the shaft, which looked sleek in published drawings, would actually have to be much bulkier to be seismically safe and stand up to high winds. University of Washington professor Al Miller, a Graham engineering consultant, worried that it would end up looking like "a stick up in the air with a big weight on the end of it." It was "clumsy looking," said Kirkwood. The tripod design was easily adapted to steel, which would be strong and could be ordered in ready-made sections that could be assembled quickly and modified as needed. Steel allowed for a faster build and a sleeker look, giving the Needle a grace that would be tough to achieve with concrete. Plus, it was more of a Space Age material. Who shot concrete into orbit?

Kirkwood remembered that Graham "looked at everything on the design board each day and suggested this and that to everybody who was there. He designed it. It wasn't somebody else." All of the collaborators felt a strong personal stake in the Needle, but Steinbrueck said of Graham, "If it hadn't been for him, there would be no Space Needle. He organized the whole thing and put it through despite the biggest obstacles you can imagine—political, economic, and technical obstacles. He's the real hero."

The Needle was also shaped by the interplay of dualities that continue to surprise. The way the tower narrows, then flares at the top, creates drama. It defies the almost universal idea that towers are masculine symbols, as the Needle also consciously incorporates feminine principles. The longer the Needle team tinkered, the better it got, and design refinements went on even as the last-minute project moved forward with increasing speed. For a 600-foot-tall tower restaurant, there were many cooks in the kitchen, but instead of spoiling the broth, they had cooked up a superb Space Age soufflé.

This model shows bright red and orange as a possible Needle color combination. Other possibilities included off-white, battleship gray, and a rainbow version.

Opposite Page
A John Graham & Co. drawing of the Needle hand-dated "26 Sept 1960" shows a mature concept of the tower.

53

The Needle became the ubiquitous symbol of the fair, as when it was used as a prop by Miss Century 21, Patricia Ann Dzejachok, who won her title competing against other female fair employees.

A huge part of the Needle collaboration also took place outside the design studio. The Space Needle represents an incredible civic effort, and a defiance of the restraints of the usual Seattle process, both the 20th- and 21st-century versions of it. The Needle was part of a large civic effort hatched by a small group that eventually inspired widespread buy-in. In a town noted for being able to gridlock or eternally second-guess even the smallest project, the Needle stands as a modern-era outlier.

The effort to launch the world's fair hit all the major civic obstacles: multiple public votes, skepticism, accusations of self-dealing, lawsuits, and concern about public funds being expended for private gain. Still, over the better part of a decade, the effort took off with support at nearly all levels of government and strong bipartisan leadership. Once the fair was a "go," it was even more necessary to create, successfully, what would be the main attraction, the media symbol, the embodiment of the entire event. The commitment to do the fair made something like the Needle imperative, which smoothed the way for it politically.

But it also raised the risk, and because it was late (the concept was unveiled and unfunded only a year and a half before opening day) and because public purses were either tapped out or extremely cautious about taking on more risk—world's fairs were notoriously chancy from a financial standpoint—failure was not an option. A failed fair, a lame symbol, could be worse than having no fair at all. Seattle could not afford a major pratfall on the global stage. Century 21's first-rate PR man Jay Rockey pointed out that all of the fair's elements were important, such as the Monorail and the Federal Science Pavilion. But it was the Needle that generated the enthusiasm and wonder. "The Needle wasn't everything, but it *seemed* like everything."

A great way to see the light-speed with which the Needle began to sprout is to check out newspaper headlines in chronological sequence:

9/12/60: "500-foot Tower Proposed for Fair"

11/1/60: "Legal Obstacles May Block Needle Bonds"

12/4/60: "Private Funds for Space Needle"

12/15/60: "Sales Agreement OK's Space Needle"

3/12/61: "4 Businessmen Will Fund Space Needle"

3/23/61: "Zone Variance Sought for Space Needle"

4/5/61: "Permit for Space Needle Recommended"

4/14/61: "Space Needle Beams Arrive"

5/22/61: "Concrete Poured: Site of Needle Dedicated"

That's seven months from the first public preview to the structure's first steel beams arriving at Pacific Car and Foundry's Structural Steel Division to be turned into Needle parts.

Artist Earle Duff captured some of the '60s glamour in this concept sketch for the Eye of the Needle restaurant. Note that the view includes a speeding jet and high-flying seagulls. What could be more Seattle?

Ground was broken on April 17 of '61 to prepare the foundation, and the official dedication and foundation concrete pour was on May 22, 11 months until opening day. In short, the Needle was able to hurdle financing, ownership, zoning, engineering, and permitting challenges and get to construction in just seven months. And it was up and running less than a year after the foundation was poured. A lot had to happen, simultaneously, to get the Needle going. This was high-speed multitasking in the age before the Internet or iPhones.

First was the funding issue. Eddie Carlson, a hotel executive, had begun to assess whether the Needle restaurant could make money, not just during the fair, but after. Would it be a viable business, like the Stuttgart Tower? Would people really pay $1 just for the privilege of riding an elevator up to a pricey restaurant? Carlson thought people would, and he began to push for his Western Hotels chain to sign on to the project. It was crucial to the plan, whether the financing was public or private, to make sure a restaurant would work. No one wanted to be saddled with a one-hit wonder, especially an empty diner in the sky.

In 1961, revolving restaurants were still novel. The turntable-on-tracks system was manufactured by Western Gear Corp. and before installation was taken for a test drive in the company's Everett parking lot.

The Needle backers also quickly tested the waters and found that neither King County nor the City of Seattle had any appetite for financing a revolving restaurant for the Fair and Civic Center. There were legal constraints, plus the fear at both the county and city levels that the taxpayers would be saddled with a "white elephant," as Seattle Buildings superintendent Fred B. McCoy called it in November 1960. The backers were looking for the city to issue revenue bonds that could be purchased by private investors to fund the Needle, and seeking what amounted to a 50-year lease to operate it on Civic Center property. At the very least, its financial stability would have to be studied.

There was also a great deal of sensitivity to the public/private nature of the fair and subsequent Civic Center. Already, critics were worried about private nest-feathering. Some critics suggested that the Civic Center concept had been hijacked by local hoteliers out to make a buck and protested federal funding of Century 21 as squandering 12.5 million taxpayer dollars on a "pipe dream."

Activists were also watchdogging and litigating over Civic Center funds and practices. A lawsuit and series of legal actions by Alfred J. Schweppe, prominent Seattle attorney and former dean of the University of Washington law school, challenged the city's use of bond funds for the Civic Center. He sought to block land condemnation for the project and also threatened legal action against city employees, actions that would have killed or delayed the fair. Legal challenges continued into 1960, even as Century 21 and Civic Center projects were under way. Anything new would likely be carefully scrutinized. According to Murray Morgan, a lawyer warned the Needle backers by laying out this scenario: "Even if the city is willing to give you a lease, just think of where you'll be if you get the thing halfway built and Al Schweppe or some cantankerous taxpayer gets a restraining order tying you up for a year or two while the courts figure out whether you're a legitimate public function." It wasn't entirely hypothetical, and no one wanted to find out the answer the hard way.

If the public wasn't going to step up to fund the Needle, then who? Bagley Wright, who was working on another project with Jack Graham, happened to see some Needle drawings in his office one day shortly after the county and city were shying away. He had been

The test was conducted with dignitaries sitting at a table while a waitress/model served coffee. The rotating ring can carry a roomful of diners quite easily with a one-horsepower motor. During the fair, one rotation took an hour, like a clock.

Needle investors Bagley Wright and David "Ned" Skinner took a helicopter over the tower's site to decide how tall to build it. Visitors to the fair could take helicopter rides over the fairgrounds and see the Needle eye-to-eye, as captured in this 1962 postcard image.

recently frustrated in one development project, and Graham encouraged him to channel his thwarted energy into the Needle project. Wright looked into it.

Wright later described himself as a young man in a hurry. In the 1960s, he was in his mid-30s and had money to invest in downtown development. In 1959, he had been a partner in the Logan Building, one of the first modern high-rise office buildings constructed in downtown since the Great Depression. The Needle seemed like a potential launchpad for future growth, a way to boost the image of Seattle as a dynamic market worthy of investment, and a fun civic project. It was "youthful optimism" that got him going, he said. He also talked about the project with Joe Gandy and, Wright later said, that "sucked me in."

Wright recruited his friend David "Ned" Skinner into the project. Skinner was involved in raising money for the fair, but he was also a respected civic leader who was known for putting money into things because it was right. "Ned Skinner really gave validity to the project," Wright said. They in turn interested the highly influential Norton Clapp, a Weyerhaeuser heir, and his aide Al Link. Jack Graham had decided to invest his time, money, and sweat; so too had Howard Wright, head of Howard S. Wright Construction, which was already the contractor on Century 21's Monorail and the Coliseum. Bagley Wright, Skinner, and Clapp each had 25 percent; Howard Wright and Graham split the other quarter share. Thus the investment group Pentagram was born, named for its five partners and headed by Bagley Wright, its youngest member (and no relation to Howard Wright). Interestingly, the fortunes that built the Needle—symbol of the Space Age—were rooted in the old Northwest economy: timber, shipping, land development, construction. Bagley Wright had sought money from others, including KING Broadcasting scion Stimson Bullitt and the head of the family that brought the aerospace industry to Seattle, the Boeings, but was turned down. It was certainly a high-risk enterprise, and not just because of the time schedule and ephemeral nature of most expo infrastructure. It was also a gamble that the fair would truly boost the business environment and that the resultant Civic Center would work as planned. None of that was guaranteed. "I was scared to death; it was more than I could afford at the time," remembered Bagley Wright.

The group of backers came together in stages, not all at once, and bank financing would also have to be secured. The banks would have to be assured the project was viable, and that would require evidence. Such one-off projects, especially those without much precedent, made them cautious. In the meantime, the Needle builders had to nail down design, costs, and other specifics, such as how tall to build it and where to build it. Word prematurely leaked that the Needle's private investors had been lined up, and that, Bagley Wright remembered, created a bit of a dilemma: They now either had to go ahead or have egg on their faces. Or both. Bagley said to Skinner, "We can build the damned thing and look up and see what fools we've made of ourselves every day, or we can leave town." They chose to stay and forge ahead.

One key decision was made when Wright and Skinner chartered a helicopter from Boeing and flew over the Century 21 site to get a sense of how high the Needle should be. The Eiffel Tower was nearly 1,000 feet high. They tested that altitude, but found the Goldilocks "just right" height at between 500 and 600 feet. Much higher, and the city became too small and impersonal, and the view of the surrounding scenery was no better. Plus, it put the Needle just higher than Queen Anne Hill, which loomed nearby. Bagley Wright was one of the city's premier arts patrons and collectors, and his discerning collector's eye helped to make just the right call. The revolving Needle restaurant would show off the region, yet keep visitors close enough to the ground to enjoy a bird's-eye view of the fairgrounds and bustling city below. Plus, a 600-foot tower was much more affordable and buildable in their time frame than anything taller.

If the city wasn't paying for the Needle, it could at least keep the skids greased to make it happen. In a desperate search for a location on or near the world's fair grounds, the city and fair organizers identified two small lots amounting to 120 by 120 feet that were city property, and thus not part of the Civic Center condemnation process. It was the site of the city's Fire Alarm Control System headquarters (address: 223 Fourth Avenue North, at Thomas Street). The site was on land once owned by the Denny family. By the turn of the 20th century, it had several homes on it whose residents and boarders included a mattress maker, a streetcar conductor, miners, and a teamster. In 1904, a fire station was erected, and later converted into the city's fire alarm HQ.

Soil tests were conducted to 150 feet on the site to see whether something of the Needle's size could be built there. It could. The test sample revealed compact glacial soil near the

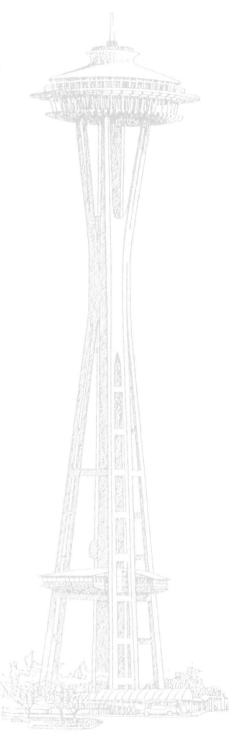

surface, about 30 feet down. "The site of the proposed 'Space Needle' is an excellent one from the standpoint of soil conditions," the soil report from Dames & Moore concluded. On February 20, 1961, the City Council approved the sale of the site to architect Jack Graham, who secured it for $75,000, the appraised value, buying it with his own cash since the Pentagram partnership had not yet been fully formed. Now, the private investors didn't have to worry about using public property and temporary leases and activist lawsuits: they could own the Needle and the land it would sit on. They'd still have to come up with the money, but they'd also have control of the property.

As the design was refined, a location was identified, and the private financing came together, a key element was making sure the Needle could get city and other approvals quickly. The area wasn't zoned for anything near as tall (the height limit was 60 feet, and the Needle would be 10 times that height), but the mayor, City Council, and city staff worked hard to cooperate. The Needle was funded with private dollars, but enabled with the help of public officials. In early February 1961, the City Council had pledged their cooperation, which included the property acquisition, base access, adjacent landscaping, and the promise of nearby parking. This vote in essence precommitted the city to provide whatever was needed to get the Needle built. In April, the Needle received a permanent (as opposed to temporary) variance. Exceptions were made on the general understanding that it was a unique project. Years later, newspaper columnist John Hinterberger wrote that while the Needle was indeed a private venture, it was also the recipient of "an exceptional amount of civic cooperation."

Underlying that cooperation was a larger-than-civic mission. The fair would boost the region's economy and image, but locals were also called to embrace newly inaugurated President Kennedy's appeal from January 1961 in which he exhorted citizens to "ask what you can do for your country." Keying off the final "clearance" for both the Needle and Monorail in April, with the one-year clock ticking, a *Times* editorial reiterated the importance of what was at stake. "This is a time of troubles for Uncle Sam," they wrote, "and of rising challenges all over the globe to things American." Century 21 had a global mission, not a provincial one. "We who are residents of the city and state that are joined with Uncle Sam in staging this exposition need to raise our sights beyond the purely local benefits. . . . All of us should realize that it is not only Seattle and state-of-Washington interest and prestige that are involved but the nation's interest and prestige as well." It was the Needle that would symbolize that message around the world.

During construction, workers found a couple of interesting things at the Needle site. A mastodon molar was dug up in the excavation, and young George Schuchart, whose father was part of the Needle investment group, remembered taking the damp, gritty relic to grade school for show-and-tell. Another find was a horseshoe. Workers reckoned that it might have come from a horse-drawn rig at the old fire station. They nailed it above the entrance to the construction shack for good luck. The Space Needle builders would need all they could get in the months ahead.

A model of the Needle photographed against a background of the fair under construction gave a rough idea of what the view might look like from the Observation Deck level.

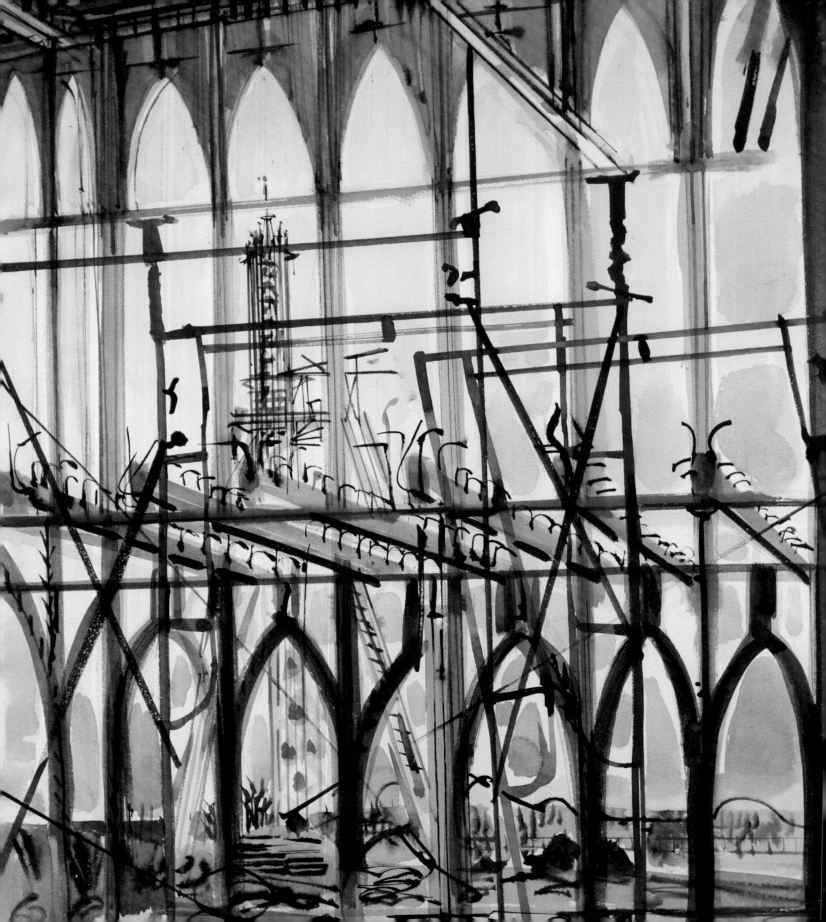

CHAPTER 4

The "400-Day Wonder"

"You will see the Needle go up and up, just like a mushroom."

— Paul Collop, Pacific Car and Foundry's Space Needle construction superintendent

Despite the fact that the Space Needle was meant to reflect a high-tech future, it was the result of some old-fashioned craftsmanship. Looking through the plans, blueprints, papers, and calculations that laid out this innovative structure is to see a precomputer world of engineering and architecture. To study how it was put together, how the steel was shaped, bolted, and snugged into place, is to realize that the Needle is a tribute to hand craft, not the computer-assisted wizardry of the real Century 21.

Going through the architectural papers, you see pencil sketches of the Needle on tracing paper, done by hand; hand-drawn schematics; artists' renderings of how the Needle was supposed to look in all its variations and iterations. No computer graphics, no 3-D software, just the work of sharp eyes and knowing hands wielding charcoal and colored pencils, building wooden models, or jotting ideas and figures on notepads.

Chief consulting engineer John K. Minasian of Pasadena, California, did the engineering calculations for the structure. The figures he came up with, the ones that have kept the Needle standing through windstorms and earthquakes for half a century, were done with pencil, paper, and slide rule. Those calculations are compiled in neat hand lettering and reflected in intricately drawn engineering plans that show every piece of the complex puzzle, and how it fits together. But they were based on an experienced tower-builder's "feel" for how to erect such structures. He practiced "sound" engineering, he'd joke: "If it sounds right . . ." Such experience would be necessary to meet the Needle's impossibly tight schedule.

The giant Needle beams shipped by rail from U.S. Steel's Chicago mill were gathered at the Structural Steel Division of Pacific Car and Foundry (now PACCAR) in Seattle. They were welded together, and holes were drilled for the 74,000 bolts that would hold it together. Some of the massive beams were bent by heating and cooling pie-shaped sections to get the perfect, graceful curves that are so distinctive. This was done in part by using methods that would have been familiar to blacksmiths and woodworkers. Pacific Car and Foundry's Bob LeBlanc, whose job was to bend the beams, described the technique as "templates, touch, and horse-sense."

Opposite Page
The construction of the Needle fascinated the city. Artists and photographers were eager to capture the event, as in this painting by Irwin Caplan that shows the Needle's then-yellow legs rising as viewed between the arches of the under-construction U.S. Science Pavilion.

The Needle was a late-bloomer. It was dedicated in May 1961, with opening day of the fair (April 21, 1962) less than a year away. David "Ned" Skinner took the stage at the ceremony.

While the Needle tower was being assembled by a seasoned crew of ironworkers, the parts were fitted by men steering sections weighing many tons into precise place, sometimes trimming down steel parts before fitting them with hand-placed bolts as they stood hundreds of feet in the air on wooden planks without nets or safety harnesses. They used gravity, cables, and fought the wind, but rapidly built the tower in much the way a kid would assemble an Erector Set. Yes, but "What an Erector Set!" exclaimed an engineer.

The companies involved—John Graham & Co., Howard S. Wright Construction Co., Pacific Car and Foundry, and all the many subcontractors and specialists—put their A-teams on the Needle project. They touted their work in trade magazines and received extensive publicity in the newspapers. U.S. Steel, which supplied the A36 carbon steel structure, took out national advertisements touting the Needle for its "sheer audacity and imagination" and called it a "400-day wonder."

Boss of the Needle erection team, Paul Collop of PACCAR, had a chatty weekly column in the *Seattle Times* documenting his crew's progress. His observations gave readers an inside view, and humanized the building of the iconic tower. Readers liked his column so much

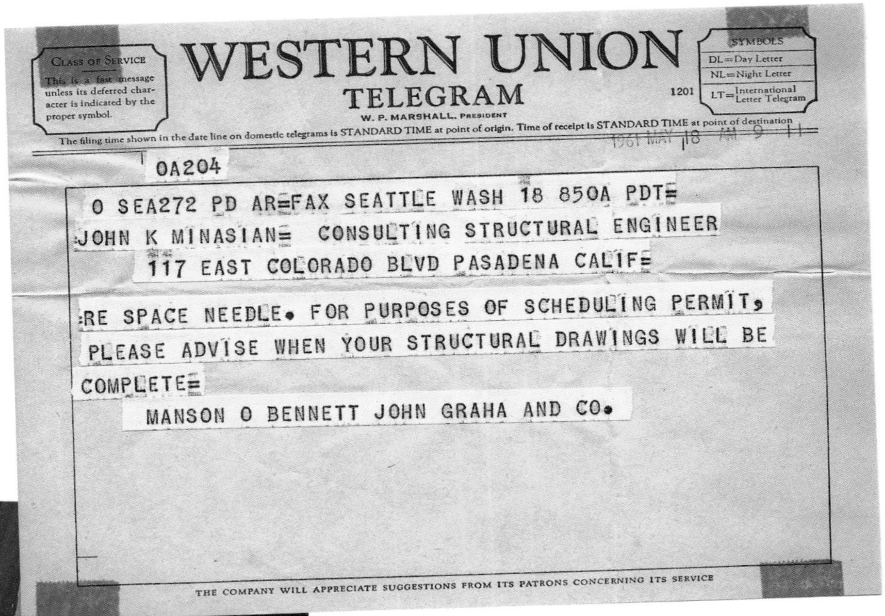

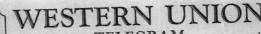

WESTERN UNION
TELEGRAM

W. P. MARSHALL, PRESIDENT

CLASS OF SERVICE
This is a fast message unless its deferred character is indicated by the proper symbol.

SYMBOLS
DL=Day Letter
NL=Night Letter
LT=International Letter Telegram

1201

The filing time shown in the date line on domestic telegrams is STANDARD TIME at point of origin. Time of receipt is STANDARD TIME at point of destination

1961 MAY 18 AM 9 11

OA204

O SEA272 PD AR=FAX SEATTLE WASH 18 850A PDT=
JOHN K MINASIAN= CONSULTING STRUCTURAL ENGINEER
117 EAST COLORADO BLVD PASADENA CALIF=

RE SPACE NEEDLE. FOR PURPOSES OF SCHEDULING PERMIT, PLEASE ADVISE WHEN YOUR STRUCTURAL DRAWINGS WILL BE COMPLETE=

MANSON O BENNETT JOHN GRAHA AND CO.

THE COMPANY WILL APPRECIATE SUGGESTIONS FROM ITS PATRONS CONCERNING ITS SERVICE

Just a few days before the dedication, John Graham & Co. architect Manson O. Bennett sent a telegram to the project's chief consulting engineer, John Minasian of Pasadena, California, to find out when the engineering drawings would be ready.

SEATTLE
WORLD'S FAIR
PREVIEW
APRIL 21 • OCTOBER 21 • 1962
CENTURY
21
EXPOSITION

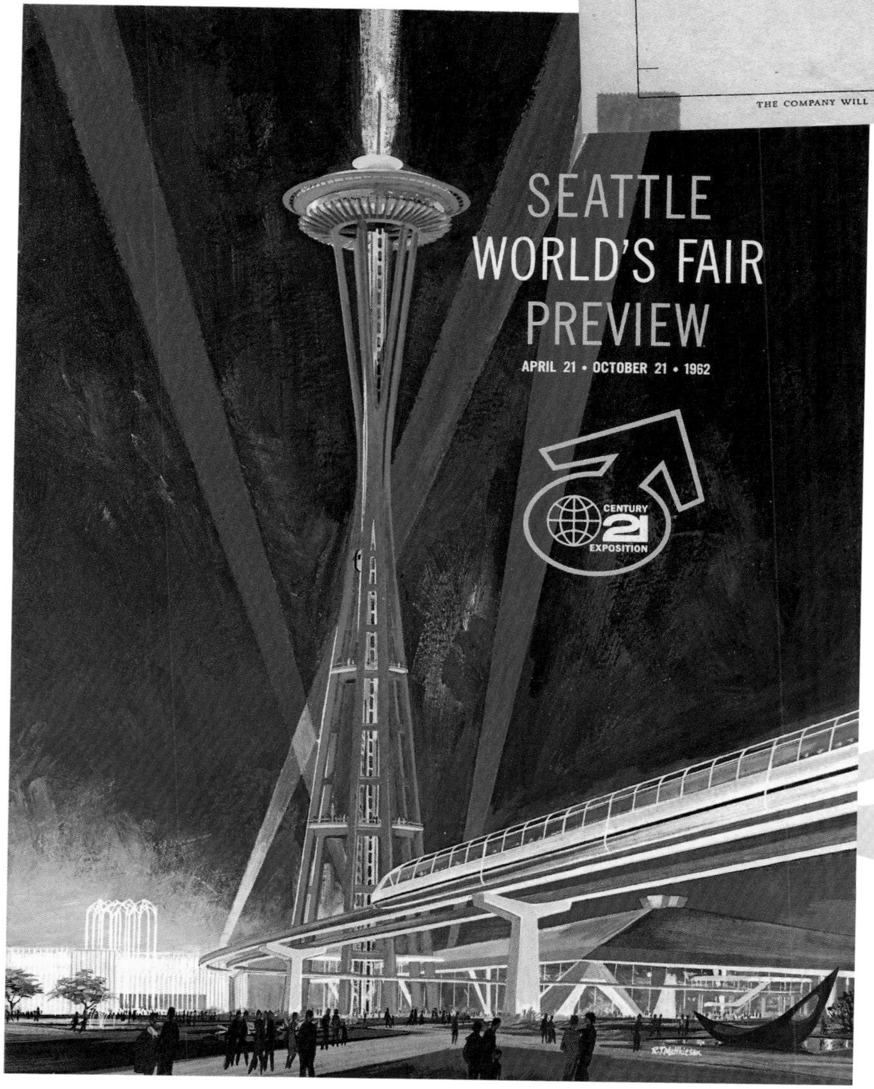

Meanwhile, the unfinished Needle was presented by artists trying to capture the spirit of the fair and future. Washington State's Department of Commerce and Economic Development produced this pre-fair brochure. It predicted that in the 21st century we'd be commuting in flying cars and wearing disposable clothes. The Needle color scheme shown here was actually considered.

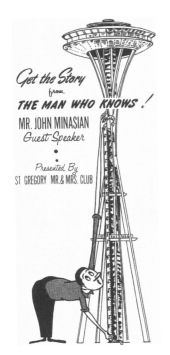

For those involved in the construction, the Needle was a point of pride. Engineer John Minasian enjoyed giving talks about how it was engineered. An experienced tower man, he had previously worked on rocket gantries for NASA as well as TV and radio towers.

It was a project to remember for the people who built it. Looking into the Needle's foundation were (from left) James Humphrey of Bethlehem Steel, Howard H. Wright, Winston Brown, president of Wright Construction, Howard S. Wright, and Lou B. Pospisil of Bethlehem Steel. The Wrights were contractors and investors in the Needle, and the family ended up owning it.

that they began sending him "Dear Abby" letters, asking him to help solve their personal problems with the same efficiency he showed in his Needle work.

The Needle might be a Space Age design, but it wasn't impersonal corporate technology. It was the work of seasoned professionals and blue-collar dads and sons. They worked at top speed and efficiency to get the project done, all feeling that it was one for the ages. Engineer Gary Noble Curtis, who worked in Minasian's office, remembered he had just read about the Needle in *Progressive Architecture* the night before the call came to his boss from John Graham & Co. asking if Minasian wanted to work on the time-squeezed project. "It was something super-special," he said. "We worked our butts off."

The Needle wasn't just a symbol of the future, or the city, but of the collective skill and know-how of its builders. Everyone saw it as a showcase for their best. The Howard S. Wright Co. invested in the Needle and supervised construction, but the Wright family expanded its personal stake in the Needle over the years and ended up owning it outright. PACCAR, famed for its truck division, made a color film, *Steel in Space*, showing off its construction work on the Needle. For John Graham & Co., the Needle demonstrated the firm's range and creativity and was highly visible in its postfair sales materials as a

The steel for the Needle was shipped by rail to Pacific Car and Foundry in Seattle, and there the parts were assembled and shaped. The curving of the giant beams was done with careful hand and eye work.

In the fall of 1961, the Needle ironworkers gathered for a group portrait at the base of the tower. Paul Collop, boss of the erection crew, is standing second from the left in the second row.

Needle workers put reinforcing steel in the Needle's 30-foot-deep foundation. Every trade involved in the project found it newsworthy. Even the publication *Fasteners* featured the Needle work on its cover.

A crowd gathered on a mound of dirt to watch as workers prepared the foundation for a massive concrete pour.

signature project. Engineer Minasian, who did projects for NASA and the military, seemed proudest of the Needle. In old age, he was rarely seen without his blue corduroy Space Needle baseball cap. The Needle is what they all remembered, and how they wanted to be remembered.

The Needle builders had to press ahead on all fronts, but they couldn't begin construction until it was fully engineered. They turned to Minasian. A man of Armenian ancestry, born in Egypt, raised in New Jersey, he was a graduate of Caltech, a consulting structural engineer who advised Lloyd's of London, and an associate professor of engineering at Los Angeles State College when he received the call to help with the Needle. Minasian was an expert at building towers. He had a hand in the construction of more than 100 TV and

Virginia Wright, the wife of Needle investor Bagley Wright, was selected to symbolically start the pouring of the concrete foundation on May 22, 1961.

Paul Collop brought his two grandsons, Steve (left) and Bob Collop, to see what was keeping their grandpa so busy in '61.

radio towers throughout the West. He had also worked on Saturn and Atlas rocket gantries and testing stands.

As the Needle tower rose, Minasian could marvel at the first successful launch of a Saturn rocket. In his papers there is a copy of the front page of the *Los Angeles Herald Examiner* for October 27, 1961, with a huge headline blaring "U.S. Launches World's Biggest Super-Rocket." It was Minasian's gantry that supported it, a steel structure as tall as a 31-story building, on wheels. It was the Saturn program that eventually put a man on the moon, a mission that President John F. Kennedy had just made a priority in May of '61, the month the Needle site was dedicated. Through Minasian, the Needle really was a product of the Space Age.

Minasian was contacted in February 1961, with construction set for May. In his handwritten notes, Minasian listed what was expected: March 1–Needle design; March 20–final mill order; March 26–rolling steel; May 1–final design of foundation; June 17–start steel erection; Nov. 1–completion of tower; Nov. 30–completion of top house. The goal was to have it ready to go by March of '62. Could it be done? It would require multitasking. Minasian would be in constant contact with Graham architects Manson Bennett and Al Fast, who were ramrodding the project. He would sometimes fly up to Seattle in the morning, meet with the Needle people, fly back to Los Angeles, and have revised drawings on Graham's desks the next morning, thanks to Special Delivery stamps in this pre-fax era. Curtis remembered that the engineers were approving plans only about 100 feet in advance of the tower-erection crew as construction commenced.

A spectacular aerial view of the tripod foundation shows more than a dozen trucks delivering their loads of concrete. Pouring the entire foundation at once was a huge undertaking, but it strengthened the Needle's base, and in the end saved time and money. It took 467 truckloads and 12 hours to deliver the 5,600 tons.

As the top was completed, a circle of exposed struts took shape as a steel sunburst familiar to all who look up from the base.

Opposite Page
As the Needle went up, the patterns of its construction came into focus. The steel core formed an interior lattice that would support the structure and carry elevators and a double helix of stairways from top to bottom.

Seattle artist Jess Cauthorn captured the drama at the Needle's base as its bright yellow legs began to rise: the cluster of vehicles, construction shacks, and the precarious "bucket" elevator that took workers up and down the tower.

After looking at the preliminary work, Minasian felt that the Needle needed to be strengthened. It could be built only once, and had to be done right, so his "sound" engineering would err on the side of safety and sturdiness. Still, the design required grace and a balance between being stiff and also flexible. After wind-tunnel tests and peer review, Minasian's Needle would have a massive foundation, putting the center of gravity close to ground level. It would be double the contemporary seismic code and built to withstand more than 100-mile-per-hour winds. Minasian had done forensic work on failed towers, and he wanted this one to be built to last. His assistant Gary Curtis later pointed out that the Needle is a very redundant structure, with its strong tripod base backed up by a very strong steel inner core.

Before Minasian was very far beyond the back-of-the-envelope phase, Graham's office was calling and asking for specifications for the steel. Curtis remembered Minasian pulling out a catalog and specifying the biggest beams they could get. The steel had to be rolled

This '62 fair poster by artist James Peck captures the drama of the mountains and makes Seattle seem like the future's base camp.

James Peck used the radiator of a construction-site truck as an easel to look at his painting of the rising tripod.

before the engineering work was finished, so they ordered parts they knew would be strong enough, and they would customize them when they got to the shop. Making the Needle strong, and getting it right the first time, was expensive. Murray Morgan estimated that Minasian's conservatism added perhaps $1 million to the cost, putting it in the $3-4 million range. Given the Needle's success, it turned out to be a bargain.

In mid-April, Howard S. Wright began to prepare the site and dig the Y-shaped, 30-foot-deep foundation. Concrete pads to anchor the Needle's massive legs were placed, along with 72 anchor bolts that were 31.5 feet long and 4 inches thick. Two hundred and fifty tons of steel reinforcements were also put in place, ready to strengthen the concrete base. Minasian wanted the foundation to be done in a single pour of concrete for greater strength, and to save time. It was said to be the largest continuous concrete pour in the West. At 5 a.m. on May 22, Howard S. Wright employee Harleigh Farwell signaled the first of 467 truckloads of concrete to be poured. At the end of some 12 hours, 5,600 tons of concrete had gone into the ground.

The Needle builders and backers used the occasion to dedicate the tower. Virginia Wright, Bagley Wright's wife, pulled a cord to symbolize the start of the work. Needle investor David "Ned" Skinner introduced the other investors. Dignitaries observed the trucks dumping their loads. Eddie Carlson later said that while watching the pour, he "cried a little" as he saw his Stuttgart obsession becoming a reality. A collection of contemporary artifacts

As the Needle rose, so did excitement about the fair. A particularly dramatic point in the construction was when the gravity-defying curved pieces that flared out were lifted and bolted into place.

and photographs was assembled for exhibit during the fair, a kind of visible time capsule of things people believed would be obsolete by the year 2000. They included an alarm clock, cigarettes, a horse with a straw hat, a mousetrap, a diet drink, a telephone, a typewriter, and—wishful thinking—an IRS tax form.

From this base, the Needle would quickly start to rise. The giant steel legs were being welded together at PACCAR, and while the city had issued a permit to start the foundation work, one had not yet been issued for the tower itself. The City Council hadn't passed the building code ordinance to allow it. But permit or not, the Needle was on its way.

The Needle's rise awakened the city to the reality of the world's fair. Public morale soared with it. Advance tickets started to sell, and by March 1962, an astonishing 3.1 million had been sold on the Needle's coattails. "I can't overstress the impact of the Space Needle," said Jay Rockey. Wrote Murray Morgan, "The Space Needle marked the turning point. The rising steel was a thermometer of civic enthusiasm. As the Needle thrust beams into the sky . . . the realization grew that there actually, really-and-truly was going to be a Seattle World's Fair." Rockey remembered that it lifted the spirits of the fair staff too, including his. "When I was feeling really down, I'd come down and look at the construction and would go away with a new state of mind. It really is going to work!"

Seattleites looked on and photographed the Needle as it rose in stages. Painters came to capture it on canvas; folks watched from their homes with binoculars. Even the Needle's high-powered originator Carlson checked progress through a telescope in his top-floor Olympic Hotel office. In a city shorter then than it is today, the Needle was visible everywhere, blocked only by the hills. It also advertised itself with steel legs painted with a highly visible bright yellow primer; the Needle's final colors were still being discussed.

The first man to put a human face on the project was Collop, boss of the tower, an experienced hand. "You name it, I worked on it," Collop said. He had worked on the Columbia River bridges, the state capitol in Olympia, Ross Dam, Civic Auditorium, the Northern Life Tower, the Tacoma Narrows Bridge, and the Colman dock ferry terminal. He'd taken some bad tumbles—including from the capitol and Colman dock—but ironwork was in his blood. As he told the *Times*' Don Duncan, "We're all just a little crazy to keep going back up. But we wouldn't want to do anything else." Still, he was extremely safety conscious, partly as a result of at least six bad falls and the many broken bones he'd suffered over the years.

The steel work began in June. The union ironworkers pulled in $3.92 per hour, and at any given time there were maybe 50 of them on the Needle. They worked in daylight, and at night inspectors went up with x-ray equipment to check the welds. The Needle had to be fit together precisely, and plumb. No one wanted the Leaning Tower of Seattle, and it was checked first thing every morning to make sure it was straight and true. The workers were lifted by a bucket called a "skip," later a construction elevator they named the Yo-Yo. The

The Needle was originally topped by a flaming natural gas torch that created a dramatic effect. It was tested on the ground, then hoisted to the top in December 1961. Ironworkers put a flag on it before it was lifted into place.

bucket offered a scary ride, as it was lifted with cable and had nothing to keep you from falling out. The German rocket scientist Wernher von Braun visited the site during construction. He was the father of the U.S. space program. He took one look at the bucket and demurred when offered a ride up the Needle. The ironworkers had to be one part monkey, one part acrobat, and a touch of astronaut.

That drama captivated people, and Collop was the designated face of the Needle, as well as its storyteller. Also problem solver. One issue that had to be resolved before the Needle rose was how to get the massive steel beams and heavy parts all the way to the top—some 600 feet in the air—when no ground-based crane could lift that high. Collop's solution was a "jumping jack," or climbing derrick crane, fitted onto the Needle's lattice steel core. This was a crane that could be hauled up the entire height of the Needle as it built the structure around itself. In the end, after the heavy, high lifting had been done, it would be lowered and removed between the Needle's beams. It was ingenious.

Now that they knew how to finish the Needle, it was time to start it. Toward the end of June, the first steel was laid and the first of the Needle's massive legs was bolted into place. These were 50-ton sections 90 feet long, and they had to be set at an angle as a tripod. Once the legs were fitted, Collop said, "then you will see the Needle go up and up, just like a mushroom."

Which is what happened. Between the end of June and early December, less than six months, the tower was raised. The worst obstacle was the wind, especially in the fall, which snagged cables, spun huge pieces of steel like tops, and threatened to blow workers off the tower. At 400 or 500 feet, a 60-mph wind was a real hazard for men who weren't strapped down. And once, as winter approached, snow at that height hampered work. Ironworker Jack Edwards, who worked on the Needle from bottom to top, remembered working on the Observation Deck halo in a snowstorm. The ironworkers were often in their own weather system. Local TV station KTNT-TV called in regular weather reports. But by and large, they worked rain or shine. And despite the speed required and the hazardous conditions, not a man was lost. Edwards remembered the worst injury to any man being a broken leg. Which wasn't the case with other Century 21 projects. At least three men were killed at other sites, including an ironworker at what was to become the Opera House.

Along the way, Seattleites were treated to stories about the construction. They watched with awe as the first "outflaring" pieces went into place in October. This was where the hour-glass Needle flared out on high, the steel beams leaning backward into empty space. The steel was tricky to shape, hard to fit, and it seemed to defy gravity. But these sturdy sections would also support the saucer filled with diners and sightseers. The first section was 54 feet long and weighed 31 tons, and had to be maneuvered into place in 20-mph winds. The ironworkers jokingly referred to those who watched from below as "sidewalk superintendents," but people wanted details on the drama in the sky.

After the tower was erected, ironworkers put out the beams of the Needle's "halo," which surrounds the Observation Deck. As was usual, the two men shown here, Jack Edwards (left) and Amby Wirkus, worked without safety harnesses.

And it was a drama. Ironworker Edwards, age 29 in 1961, was what was called a "connector," one of the men who positioned the steel parts into place and did the preliminary bolting. They eschewed safety harnesses and nets because they had to be nimble to avoid being whipped by deadly cables or crushed by swinging beams. The men didn't want to trip over or be tied down by ropes when they needed to move fast. And they carried a fair amount of weight on them, which could make mobility a challenge until you got used to it. A connector's loaded tool belt weighed between 10 and 15 pounds, plus a worker might be carrying an 8-pound maul or heavy pry bar.

As the Needle rose, those who'd worked on it the longest became accustomed to the heights. Edwards said his day often began at 3 a.m., when the new steel was delivered, while the roads were empty of traffic. The workdays ended at 4:30 p.m., and he liked the overtime pay. Some men who joined the project late, he said, had trouble getting their balance and bearings so high in the sky, and quit after only a day. In the cold weather, Edwards said, they sometimes took nips from a thermos of rum-laced tea. "I'm afraid of heights," Edwards said, "but I respect them."

Before the ironworkers wrapped up their work, they accomplished a Needle first: On December 2, they partook of the first dinner ever served on the still-unfinished tower. Collop arranged for a caterer, Bill Hewitt, to come up to the windblown platform that would become the base of the restaurant, and serve a full dinner buffet for the crew. The event received front-page coverage: "First Meal Atop Needle, Was the Salad Ever Tossed! Ironworkers Dine High." The menu: "roast young Washington turkey, whipped potatoes and giblet gravy, cranberry sauce, fruit-and-cottage-cheese tray, hot orange rolls, green beans

The first dinner on the Needle was a buffet served to workers on the unfinished and open top house in December 1961. No rotating restaurant, but excitement was provided by gusts of wind that tossed green salad over the side.

A worker guides a giant leg beam into place. The Needle was bolted together, and the holes had to line up exactly.

A *Life* magazine cover featuring the Needle nearing completion stirred up excitement as a national audience saw the structure take shape.

Needle workers constructing the top house had to swing pieces of steel into place that were lifted by cables, tricky work in the winds at 500 feet.

with almonds and mushrooms—even pumpkin pie and whipped cream." Said Collop, "We couldn't wait for the official opening—not this gang of ironworkers who have labored long and hard to push this Tower of Babel almost 600 feet into the air. One thing was certain: *We* were going to have the first meal served in the Eye of the Needle, even if it meant cooking it with a welding torch." It could be said that the meal was shared with the whole city, as gusty winds took away the salad course and whipped cream.

With the ironworkers wrapping up, the top house was now the priority, and the Needle swarmed with men, including carpenters, electricians, elevator installers, and other specialists whose job was to construct and finish the five-story building that sits atop the tower. The top house included the restaurant, a mezzanine level for the kitchen, the observation deck, and utility and elevator equipment rooms at the very top. Instead of 50 ironworkers climbing the length of the tower, the Needle platform often had more than 100 workers who were trying to get it ready and finishing the core, which included a double-helix set of stairways, utilities, and the elevator equipment. The place was abuzz, with workers representing up to 15 trades at one time. There was some frustration at one point, when ironworkers walked off the job for a half-hour work stoppage in a dispute with the carpenters over work on the platform floor. It was resolved quickly. It was important too: As part of the BIE agreement to officially recognize the fair, organizers had promised there would be no labor problems in Seattle. But the minor dispute marked a major advance for the Needle.

FIRM COPY

INSPECTION REPORT

Date __January 2, 1962__ , 195__

Firm name __PACIFIC CAR & FOUNDRY__   Firm address __120 West Hudson, Seattle__

Location of this operation __Space Needle__   Type of operation __5-8__

Is there an organized safety committee __x__   Safety engineer __x__   Both____

First aid equipment __Good__   First aid station____   Sanitation __Good__

General condition of equipment __Good__

Housekeeping __Good__   Work order issued____

Note number____

Item No.	Remarks:
	We wish to extend our congratulations on a hazardous job well done!
	Also our appreciation for your cooperative attitude toward the State
	Safety Division.

DEPARTMENT OF LABOR AND INDUSTRIES
DIVISION OF SAFETY

WALTER SMITH
GENERAL SAFETY INSPECTOR

PHONE MAIN 3-2350
1401 2ND AVENUE
SEATTLE, WASHINGTON

Firm____

By____

Title____

S. F. No. 8355—2-55—50M. 40765.

DEPARTMENT OF LABOR AND INDUSTRIES
SAFETY DIVISION
By _Walter Smith_
Walter Smith   Inspector

Leave card with this report.

The Needle didn't lose a man during construction, and this state inspection report at the completion of the tower phase recognized "a hazardous job well done!"

The June-July 1962 issue of *Westward*, a magazine produced by Kaiser Steel, touted the use of "The Miracle Metal of Century 21." An article stated that the steel Needle had a "beauty no photograph can convey." So for their cover, they turned a black-and-white picture into a painting that brightened the future.

It occurred on December 14, the day a Howard S. Wright steeplejack named Bob Kessler, dressed as Santa, climbed the newly installed torch and officially crowned the tower construction by placing a Christmas tree on top of what was now the West's tallest building.

Meanwhile, things were busily being readied on the ground. Western Hotels was contracted to design and operate the restaurant and run the Needle, from elevators to gift shops. They had to begin interviewing potential staff, plan menus, and create a world-class dining establishment that was unlike any other in the country: a 260-seat rotating restaurant over 500 feet in the sky that would have to show off the best of the Northwest to an international audience.

The first choice for the restaurant's name was "Top of the Needle," but the public didn't like it, many thinking it was too derivative of San Francisco's hotel view dining room, Top of the Mark. Eye of the Needle was the popular, punning replacement. People wanted something that was one-of-a-kind. An interior color scheme was selected: rich earth tones, browns, oranges, and golds. Uniforms were designed for each staff position, including hostesses in gold lamé. The Needle designers tapped local industrial designer Gideon Kramer for a modern type of molded fiberglass chair that stood on a Needlelike metal base. It was called the Ion chair, and the Needle made it world famous, an icon of modern design. The chairs were handmade, and Kramer and his family remembered sitting around the dinner table sanding the wooden armrests to get the commission done in time for the fair.

The Needle's final colors were also becoming apparent. Graham's team had considered a number of schemes, including "international orange" (color of the Golden Gate Bridge) with a yellow top. Architect Steinbrueck was consulted and recommended the shades "clover white" and "charcoal gray" from Rust-Oleum samples. One Graham color rendering showed a rainbow color scheme starting with white at the base, shifting to yellow, orange, and then red at the top. In the fall of 1961, it was announced that an off-white had been chosen, and the final supports at the top of the tower were painted that color in the shop before they were lifted into place. Soon, the bright yellow primer on the base would be covered, and the top house was painted a bright tangerine, what some called "Howard Johnson's orange." Hoge Sullivan, the Needle's manager, gave Space Age names to the various colors: Astronaut White for the tower, Orbital Olive for the core, Re-Entry Red for the halo, and Galaxy Gold for the sunburst and roof.

Perhaps the most important component for the top house was the restaurant's turntable. A 14-foot-wide section of the outer dining room floor would rotate once per hour. Graham designed it; Western Gear of Everett built, tested, and installed it; and remarkably, a full dining room with tables, chairs, guests, and staff could be turned with only a one-horsepower motor.

Another key Needle component was a giant torch to top it off. Instead of installing a TV tower, it was decided to light up the Needle with a natural gas flame on the roof. At the tip of the torch would be a required red aircraft beacon to satisfy the FAA and local pilots who were concerned that the Needle would be a navigational hazard. Below the beacon, the torch would be lit at night by gas lines that were coming up to serve the kitchen anyway, and only had to be extended to the pinnacle. Washington Natural Gas undertook the project. One hitch, according to Graham architect Rod Kirkwood, was that the gas company paid only for getting the line to a structure, not the interior lines. However, the builders persuaded them to regard the line to the top of the Needle as a "vertical street main," since the building being served was the top house. The tower was like the street to get there.

In those pre-energy-conservation times, the gas company boasted that the torch burned enough gas per hour to heat 125 average homes. The torch frame was a tripod, kind of a mini-Space Needle on top of the Needle. Seattle writer Bill Speidel likened it to a Bunsen burner on "a magnificent scale."

Before it was even hooked up or lit up, however, there was a bit of controversy. The ironworkers had lifted it to the top house, and in their tradition attached an American flag to it. But when the Needle was topped with a Christmas tree, Collop took umbrage at the displacement of the American flag. A tree, he said, was an "idea that comes from Norway or Sweden, where they put a tree on top of a new house." That just wouldn't do, he said, unless perhaps the Needle "were being built in Ballard."

The folks who helped to build the Needle all had strong feelings about it, and a sense of ownership and pride in it, from designers to owners to engineers to ironworkers. It had captivated the city too, with Seattleites debating and second-guessing every decision, from its colors to its lighting to the dining room's name. But as the winter of '62 turned to spring, the Needle was readying itself for its international debut at the world's fair. If Seattleites were already embracing the Needle, letting it lift their excitement for the big event to come, what would the rest of the world think of it? They were about to find out.

Workers swarm the top house to get it ready in early 1962. In fact, work was finished early enough that the Observation Deck was opened to the public in March, nearly a month before the fair officially opened.

CHAPTER 5

The Needle Goes Around the Globe

"There will be Space Needles cropping up all over after the success of this one."

— Walt Disney

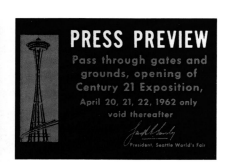

The Century 21 staff did an extraordinary job of getting publicity for the fair, and giving the media a sneak preview ensured timely stories about its official opening.

In the spring of 1962, Seattleites lined up for the World's Fair, the Century 21 Exposition. This fair wasn't the Puyallup. Visitors were off to meet the future, so they left their jeans at home and put on a suit or a dress. Everyone was advised to bring good walking shoes. The fair site was small—only 74 acres—and had been called a "jewel box" or "transistorized," but people would be on their feet all day, walking and standing in lines, mostly on hard concrete. Imagine for a minute that you are back in time, making a first visit to the amazing new Space Needle at the fair . . .

Despite all the new parking lots near the site, you sensibly take the bus downtown, then walk to a nearby bank and pick up some large brass World's Fair "dollars," which local merchants accept as real money. They're heavy in your hand, but somehow, like poker chips in a casino, easier to spend.

You cross Pike Street and join the crowds at Westlake, now dominated by a huge covered Monorail terminal where the Red and Blue Alweg trains are filled to capacity shuttling guests to the fair site along a raised concrete track a little over a mile long. If you're lucky, you get a seat near the driver, far forward, where you have a sensation of speed as you glide down Fifth Avenue. You're seeing Seattle from an entirely new angle, sliding by the upper-story windows of nearby buildings, zipping through air without the clanking and rattling of old-fashioned rail, and with no stoplights. At the end of the ride looms the symbol of the fair, the amazing, slender hourglass Space Needle.

The Needle and Monorail have become symbols of the fair, impressed on the national consciousness by a recent cover photograph on Life *magazine that showed the Monorail racing off the page as the Needle is lit up in the background with a flaming torch on top. The Monorail lets you out at the Needle's base, and first thing, you head to buy a ticket to take you to the top. Like most fairgoers, you want to see the Needle more than anything, but many visitors will never get to the top. It'll cost $1, over and above your entrance fee to the fair, to ride to the Observation Deck. If you have lunch at the Eye of the Needle restaurant, there's a $2 minimum, $5 at dinner. Menu prices are about on a par with those of Seattle's best restaurants, such as Canlis or Trader Vic's.*

But the Needle's popularity is huge. The newspapers say that over 10,000 guests per day are whizzing up and down in the gold capsulelike elevators. The Needle takes no reservations

Opposite Page
A first view of the Needle from the base gave visitors a look at the final colors, including its gold capsule elevators, and the speakers for the electronic carillon music that turned the Needle into a giant bell tower for the duration of the fair.

The Needle was a hit from day one, and lines were long. The trip to the top was $1, and lunch at the revolving Eye of the Needle restaurant was a $2 minimum, first come, first served. Waits of three hours, rain or shine, were not uncommon.

(except for an 8 a.m. breakfast seating). For the most part, it's first come, first served. Seattle is an egalitarian town; rich and poor must wait in line. Unless you're a VIP, in which case you are smuggled to the top in the slow-moving service elevator from the basement. The Needle's operators keep this service low-profile so as not to infuriate folks who have been waiting for two or three hours, sometimes in the rain. When it's hot, the Needle staffers carry smelling salts to revive old folks who faint in the heat during the wait.

Because of the rush schedule and cost, the landscaping at the base of the Needle is spare. There is no fancy entryway with a spiraling ramp for those waiting to ascend. You walk up stairs right to the Needle's base, buy your ticket, and get in line. Later in the fair there will be 250 modern Ion chairs set up outside for the people who've been waiting the longest. Guests will scoot from seat to seat as each elevator load goes up until it's their turn. But for now, those in

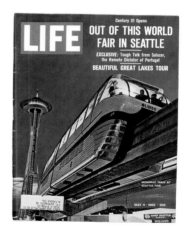

Feeding the Needle with guests was the Monorail, which picked up passengers downtown at Westlake and whisked them to the fairgrounds, as it still does today.

line are guided into a series of metal and chain barriers called "the maze." The only fun part is the anticipation. At least most people are polite and patient. When the Eiffel Tower opened in 1889, the papers were filled with stories about people shouting complaints about the wait.

It's noisy at the base. You noticed that when you stepped off the Monorail. Crowds are good sized, and you can hear music in the distance. The fair's marching band might be coming by. A sightseeing helicopter is taking off and landing from the roof of the old Armory, now called the Food Circus, giving people a whirlybird's-eye view of the fair. The jabber of voices and foreign languages around you adds to the sensation of being in an exotic bazaar. The Needle staff speaks 11 different languages.

SPACE TOWER, 550 feet in height, is crowned by a restaurant and observation deck which revolves 360 degrees per hour to present an ever-changing panorama of Seattle, Puget Sound and nearby mountain ranges.

HI-SPEED MONORAIL, the world's first, whisks visitors from downtown Seattle to the Exposition grounds . . . more than a mile . . . in just 96 seconds. Century 21 visitors will thrill to this premiere full-scale operation of a high-speed, mass transportation system of the future.

The Needle and Monorail went hand-in-hand, and the Howard S. Wright Co. was the general contractor on both projects, as well as the Coliseum. The Monorail delivered passengers to the Needle's base.

To add to the din, the Needle has been turned into a giant bell tower. An electronic carillon with over 500 bells has been installed. A carillon was a popular feature at the 1958 fair in Brussels. At ground level, there's a concrete box that houses the device, and you can peer through picture windows and watch the carillonneurs play. The signals are transmitted to more than 40 giant speakers placed high on the Needle, and at intervals they blast music that can be heard 10 miles away or more.

The fair is a stage set of exotic Space Age shapes and colors; the rides of the Gayway are in constant motion. Near the Needle is the Pavilion of Electric Power, in the shape of a giant hydroelectric dam. All of it generates excitement and anticipation, which makes waiting in line

Another great way to see the fair was to take the Union 76 Skyride across the fairgrounds.

hard, but people are traveling from all over to get up there. John Wayne was an early visitor, as were the Shah and Empress of Iran. Literally and figuratively, the Needle is the fair's pinnacle, a celebrity magnet in a town with very few celebrities, unless you count Bobo, the Woodland Park Zoo's gorilla.

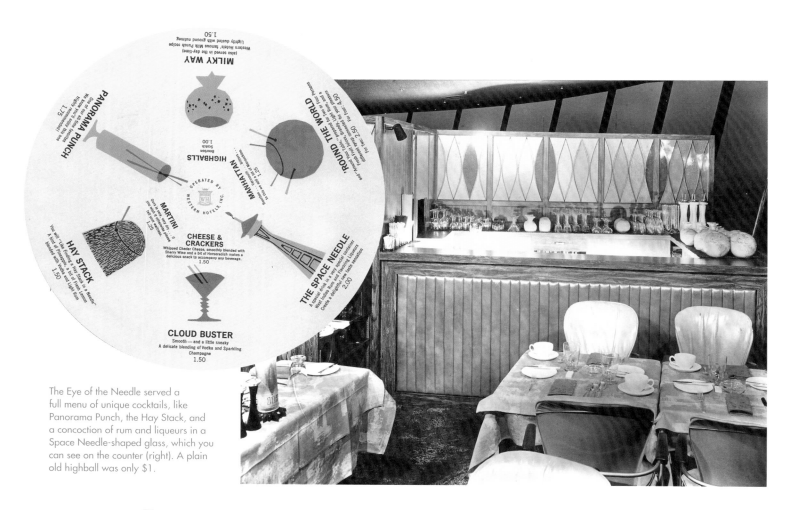

The Eye of the Needle served a full menu of unique cocktails, like Panorama Punch, the Hay Stack, and a concoction of rum and liqueurs in a Space Needle-shaped glass, which you can see on the counter (right). A plain old highball was only $1.

A writer from National Geographic described meeting the Needle for the first time: "Standing at the foot of the Needle, I was reminded of the Eiffel Tower, but where the Parisian landmark dwindles to a point on top, the Space Needle spreads its broad disk, as if offering man a home in the sky. Stepping into a capsule-like elevator . . . we had the feeling of shooting into space."

Finally, it's your turn to shoot to the top. You and a group of 28 other people jam into the little windowed elevator for your 48-second rocket ride. The elevator operator is a beautiful uniformed gal who happens to be tall. All of them are 5 feet 6 inches or taller. One, Linda Humble, was just named Miss Seattle. As the elevator rises, passengers gasp. You see the fair pulling away, you feel the motion in your stomach, you notice that the doors, if they opened, would leave you staring into empty space.

You've decided you cannot miss a meal at the Needle. Who has eaten in a restaurant that goes around in a circle? No one you know. "Dining a la dervish," Life magazine called it. Will you get seasick? How will the waitress ever find your table after taking your order? Can you afford it? You've read a little bit about the food in the newspapers. One story said that when the Shah and Empress of Iran had lunch at the Needle, they ate "Dungeness crab legs on ice, green salad, filet mignon, peas, artichokes, potato gems, strawberries and coffee." That sounds awfully good to you.

The restaurant's interior color scheme featured earthy browns, oranges, and golds, including hostesses in gold lamé uniforms. Patrons had to get used to eating in a dining room that rotated. Once in a while guests' coats and purses would be lost if left on the windowsill, and waitresses had to keep track of patrons, who were constantly on the move.

A hostess takes you to your table, luckily on the outer rim, with a spectacular view. It takes you a few minutes to get oriented. The table is stationary, but you are in motion as the dining room turns at the stately pace of one revolution per hour (it's true—some guests have even timed it). It would be a very slow dervish indeed. Strangers sometimes leave funny little notes on the windowsill, and you can read them as you pass by while eating up the view. Once in a while someone loses a purse or coat by leaving it on the sill. It's hard to remember you're in a restaurant that can carry you away from your belongings.

The cocktail menu is orange and circular, the color and shape of the Needle's top if you were looking down on it. On one side, it tells you what you're seeing out the window in every direction—Magnolia, Puget Sound, Mount St. Helens. On the other, it lists exotic-sounding drinks like the Hay Stack (get it, a Hay Stack in a Needle?), which features pineapple, lemon, vodka, and light rum, or a Cloud Buster, with vodka and champagne. On a budget? Highballs are $1.

These Needle-stemmed champagne glasses were created for the VIP opening of the Needle on the eve of the fair.

One thing you notice on the menu: local foods are favored, along with an international flair. Crab, Alaskan shrimp, Puget Sound salmon, apple pie made from Washington apples with Tillamook cheese from Oregon. You've never heard the 21st-century term "locavore," but you could be one at the Needle.

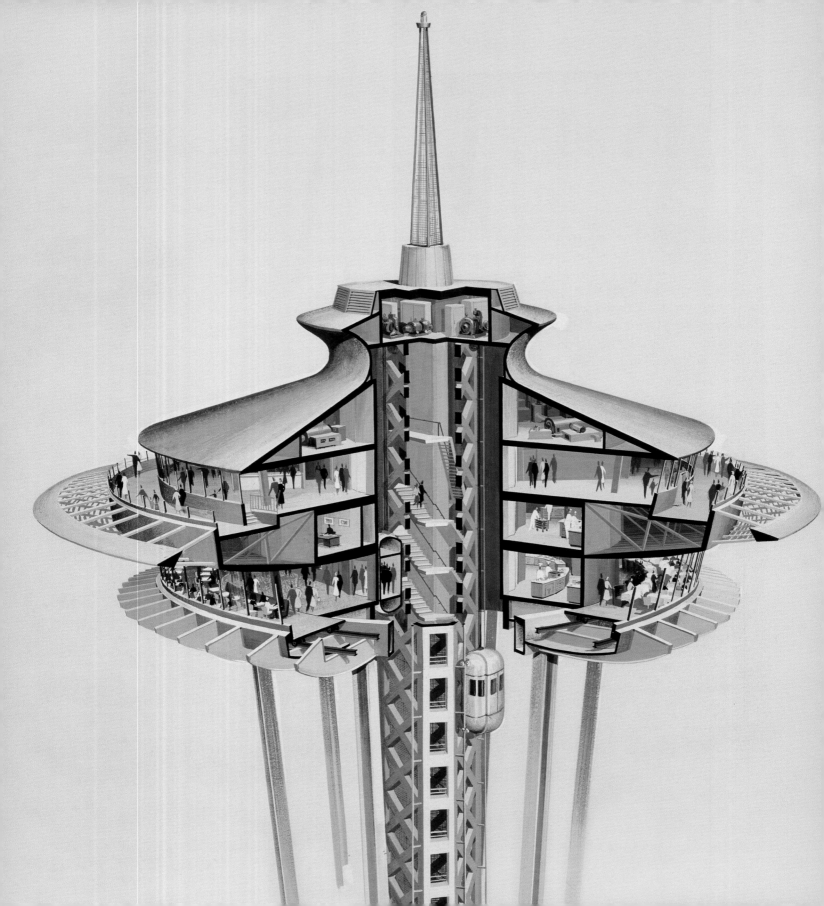

You can order a good steak, but also dishes with curry, or a French preparation. For a simple lunch, you can get a corned beef sandwich for $2. For a blow-out dinner like the Shah's, you order fresh crab legs ($1.75), a romaine salad with chopped herring ($1), filet mignon ($5.75), fresh strawberries marinated in kirsch with meringue and whipped ice cream ($1.25), and custom-blended coffee (25 cents), plus a bottle of Louis Martini Burgundy from California ($3.35). You can even take home an embossed souvenir menu (50 cents). This dinner for two is pricey, over $25. Consider that fairgoers spend an average of only $6.59 per day per person total. But, like 92 percent of Needle diners surveyed during the fair, you think it was worth it.

One thing you notice: your waitress always manages to find you, no matter where your table has turned to. The seating sections are color-coded and named after Mounts Rainier, Adams, St. Helens, and Baker, the big Cascades volcanoes. A clocklike device near the kitchen tells the staff which section is where as the restaurant rotates. The waitresses' uniforms are subtly color-coded by section too. You're not aware of this, so it's a bit like magic. And speaking of magic, you see something very strange. Maybe the Cloud Buster went to your head. A Needle staffer brings a Pacific Northwest Bell telephone to the neighboring table so the guest can make a call, but the phone is cordless. How did they do that? Maybe someday, we'll all have cordless phones 600 feet in the air!

The Eye of the Needle attracted plenty of VIPs, none more powerful than some of the politicians who made the fair possible. Shown here are (from left) Sen. Warren G. Magnuson, Washington governor Albert Rosellini, Jermaine Magnuson, and Sen. Henry M. "Scoop" Jackson.

Opposite Page
The Needle's top house is essentially a five-story building on a tripod. The levels are the restaurant, a mezzanine with kitchen facilities, the Observation Deck, and floors for utilities and elevator equipment. This rendering was produced to give fairgoers a cutaway look at the saucer's inner operations.

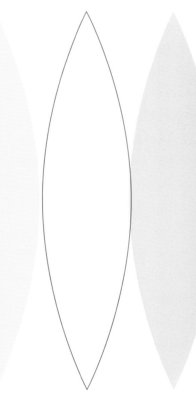

The Needle was a backdrop for the Plaza of the States, where many fair ceremonies took place. Each state had a day at the fair, and state and foreign delegations were invariably taken up the Needle and given VIP treatment.

The Needle inspired fashion. Here, Donna Edgin, a telephone operator for Howard S. Wright Co., models a Space Needle hairdo by Mr. Paul (Robert Paulson) for the Washington State Hairdressers' Association show. Her hair was dyed blue and white and swept up around a plastic model of the Needle.

Time for a postprandial stroll. You might hop off the merry-go-round and head upstairs to the Observation Deck. It's packed with people. Inside there's a crowd buying pens, colorful plates, and other Space Needle souvenirs. You can ring your grandmother in Cincinnati from one of a dozen pay telephones installed for that "guess where I'm calling from, Ma" phone call. Eleven-year-old George Schuchart, whose father was part of the Needle investment group, remembered calling his mother in Seattle and "shouting into the phone as if I were on the moon," so novel and remote did a call from the Needle to earth seem.

You can buy the brand-new U.S. stamp featuring the Space Needle and Monorail (a cheap souvenir at 4 cents). There's a U.S. Post Office downstairs, where your postcard or envelope will be canceled "Space Needle, WASH." The first letter from the Needle was sent by Senator Warren G. Magnuson to President John F. Kennedy. The senator wrote an invitation on the envelope: "Come to the fair."

The outdoor deck extends all the way around, and on a classic spring day, the sun is playing peekaboo, the mountains too. The most popular view isn't west to the Sound or east to the Cascades, but south. That's where the most-used coin-operated telescope is. From there, you can see the Smith Tower, downtown, and weather permitting, Mount Rainier.

Seattle looks so different from up here. Queen Anne Hill seems flatter. The city looks like a toy town, the cars like bugs and buses like caterpillars, Lake Union a place for bathtub toys. You can see flat roofs and parking lots, the traffic on Highway 99. In the distance, you see the new I-5 freeway slicing along Capitol Hill. A policeman on "space patrol" monitors traffic and parking with a pair of binoculars and a walkie-talkie. He can even see well enough to radio down so they can ticket jaywalkers.

Directly below are the stark white Gothic arches and serene pools of the Federal Science Pavilion glittering in the sun and echoing the snowy Olympics behind them. You can see the Gayway rides and Union 76 Skyride, Memorial Stadium with its water-ski show, and the pyramid they call the Coliseum, which sits like a squat concrete temple. The fair is like a huge mechanical toy with lights and many moving parts. Except for a waist-high railing and a chest-high glass screen, there is nothing between you and the city except a halo of louvers that encircle the deck. Being out on the Needle is exhilarating, but it feels a little precarious too. The Needle looks so delicate from below. Will it snap off? Will it take off? The saucer is hovering over the city, and you feel like an alien seeing it for the first time.

A U.S. first-class postage stamp (letter rate: 4 cents) issued for the fair featured the Needle and Monorail. A special post office was opened at the Needle, where mail was postmarked "Space Needle, WASH."

A fanciful foreign postcard got the Needle's color and the fair's geography wrong, but captured the festive spirit of Century 21 and Seattle's new landmark.

If the world's fair put Seattle on the map, the Space Needle was the pin in that map. The world was coming to Seattle, and the Needle was the number-one symbol pointing the way.

Seattleites had embraced the Needle at birth and wove it into popular culture, from hairdos and high fashion to songs and poetry. Newspaper photographers had popularized views from the Needle's heights. When the Needle's tower was erected and deemed safe enough, reporters were allowed up. Paul Collop had refused to put any women on the Needle job—there was no ironworker equivalent of Rosie the Riveter on this project. But one account that broke a barrier was when the *Seattle Post-Intelligencer*'s Eleanor Bell went up in early December 1961, claiming to be the "first of the weaker (?) sex at the top." Her story would soon be the familiar experience of many local fairgoers who would feel how the Needle was changing their sense of the city and region.

"It was a wonderful sight," Bell wrote. "I could look down on the Smith Tower, Queen Anne Hill and the TV towers were out there below. I could see Bellevue, Redmond, Everett, Green Lake, and Tacoma's smokestacks and smelters in the distance. Kirkland was hidden by haze. So was Mt. Rainier. I saw the shiny West Seattle water tower, Pier 91, hospitals, factories, the whole city and adjoining cities all around. And almost close enough to touch, it seemed, the blue and white sky."

A few folks got sneak previews by sneaking around. One was Junius Rochester, son of fair organizer Al Rochester. Junius got a job at the exhibit for the upcoming New York World's Fair. One day before the Needle was finished or the fair opened, he and a couple of young women who worked with him walked onto the construction site and found an unlocked gated door leading to a stairway. With no one to stop them, they walked up the 800-plus steps of one of the Needle's newly finished stairways. On the way up, one of the women lost an earring, and they could hear it cling-clanging for a long time as it dropped down the steel core. When they opened the door at the top, Rochester recalled, a uniformed guard said, "For God's sake, where did you come from?" They told him they had just walked up from the bottom, and he said that had never happened before.

The Needle was being readied for opening day of the fair, April 21, 1962. But in fact, it opened early. The staff of some 300 would have to be trained, so the Needle embarked on a shakedown cruise. The investors also wanted to start generating revenue to cover their costs. Opening early was an opportunity, as Space Needle president Bagley Wright later recalled, to "see if anyone would come."

The Needle and Monorail both opened on March 24, 1962, almost a month before the fair. That first day, a Saturday, only one of the Needle's passenger elevators, the one known as the Blue elevator, was working, and the restaurant would remain closed to the public until the fair opened. But visitors could take the Monorail from Westlake and access the Century 21 site for an early look-see from the Observation Deck. Needle assistant manager Claude Wakefield Jr. remembered going up with the first load of visitors that day.

They were mostly the families of members of the construction crew, he said. "Suddenly the word raced throughout the city and throughout the state yesterday," reported the *P-I*. "'The Space Needle is open at the World's Fair. Grab the kids and let's go.' And that's just what thousands of families did." Bagley Wright could breathe a sigh of relief at the long lines.

This was the Needle's first test run, and it was dubbed a success. The day was blustery, the top house full of construction clutter. Howard S. Wright construction boss Harleigh Farwell dubbed it "quite a day," according to the *Times*. "As if by magic, the sun burned through the rain clouds exactly at noon. Elliott Bay glistened. Shadows etched the skyline." One visitor, Viola Shields, said, "This certainly beats the Eiffel Tower."

By Sunday, a second elevator was operating, and they both worked hard. The Needle stayed open during the week in the evenings, 5 p.m. to 8 p.m., with extended all-day weekend hours. On the weekend of April 7-8, the newspapers estimated, the Needle had 22,000 visitors in two days. The Observation Deck souvenir shop did a brisk business (the most popular item was a button saying "I was there—Space Needle 1962"), and the Needle worked out a few bugs. The very first weekend, a visitor walked through a glass door and cut her thumb. Safety glass was promptly installed to prevent future accidents.

The world's fair staff was happy about the success, but they worried that too many people were getting onto the unfinished fair site, interfering with last-minute work. Organizers also didn't want to spoil the novelty of Opening Day. They pressured the Needle to restrict

Many fair visitors came by car, and the Needle acted as a beacon on gas station maps.

access. If the trial run was any indicator, the Needle was going to be a smash. Hoge Sullivan estimated that an astonishing 110,000 people had visited the Observation Deck *before* opening day of the fair.

The restaurant was also being readied. On April 12, the first meals were served in the Eye of the Needle. It was lunch in two shifts for 200 employees, including waitresses, hostesses, and bartenders. Everyone got the chance to greet, seat, and serve "guests." Western Hotels chef Rene Schiess oversaw the Needle's menu and made sure that everything on it was available. The Needle had given itself a challenge by putting a first-class restaurant in rotation on a disk nearly 600 feet in the air. There was little storage or freezer space—food and supplies had to be brought up from below. The kitchen itself was more like a ship's galley. And under these conditions, showcase fare had to be prepared. Schiess had worked in kitchens around the world, from France and Istanbul to Seattle's Olympic Hotel, and this one posed challenges. But for guests, such challenges wouldn't matter. The service and food promised to be top-notch, however difficult it would be for the staff to prepare and serve.

Rooting for the Needle staff were the folks from the Eiffel Tower. The head of their restaurants, André Pignarre, had offered to bring an entire kitchen crew to Seattle to prepare the Needle's opening-day dinner, if only they would kindly send a Boeing 707 to fly them in. Western Hotels and Eddie Carlson politely declined. In the spring of 1961, fair organizers had held a special VIP dinner in Seattle as a belated tribute to the Eiffel Tower's 70th birthday, and the menu was designed by Pignarre, who also sent Bordeaux, cognac, and liqueurs from the Eiffel Tower's own "caves" for the pleasure of the "space tower" gourmets.

There was a common understanding that these two landmarks, old and new, were related by expositions, technology, novelty, the future, urban identity, and world-class food. The Eiffel Tower restaurants put up Century 21 posters to promote the fair. And at 12:46 a.m. on April 21, 1962, the Needle was christened by a representative of Paris, Mrs. Robert Petin, who smashed a bottle of Eiffel Tower champagne on the Observation Deck railing. Fair organizers then toasted with special champagne glasses featuring amber-colored Space Needle stems.

France was the largest foreign exhibitor at the fair, the Paris-based BIE had made the fair possible, and French cuisine still set the culinary standards to which the Needle aspired. Bagley Wright remembered lunching at the Needle during the fair with Time-Life mogul Henry Luce and fair architect Paul Thiry. Luce was grumpy, Wright said, because all through the meal Thiry, whose parents were Parisians, lectured Luce about how everything great in America came from France. The bottom line was that the Eiffel Tower acknowledged the Needle as a kindred spirit.

The six months of the Seattle World's Fair embedded the Needle as a world icon. It was featured on network TV, radio, and hundreds of magazine covers. It was covered by national and international newspapers and even turned up in a *New Yorker* cartoon and a Walt Disney comic book. While the Eye of the Needle revolved, it's also accurate to say that the whirl of the fair revolved around the Needle. Foreign translators at the fair reported that the first question asked in any language was about the Needle.

The demand to get up the tower was huge and relentless: corporate executives, celebrities, media people all asked for VIP treatment. Bagley Wright said he was never so popular as during the fair, when he and his wife, Virginia, could use their influence to get a table for friends. The list of celebrity visitors was long: world leaders and political figures like the Shah and Empress of Iran, Prince Philip of Great Britain, Robert F. Kennedy and his clan, Richard Nixon and his family, Vice President Lyndon Johnson, New York governor Nelson Rockefeller, and U.S. United Nations ambassador Adlai Stevenson; media figures such as Edward R. Murrow, Walter Cronkite, columnist Drew Pearson, radio host Paul Harvey, and *Life*'s Luce; celebrities, artists, and entertainers like Roy Rogers and Dale Evans, Merv Griffin, Elvis Presley, Danny Kaye, John Wayne, Carol Channing, George Burns, Henry Mancini, Leontyne Price, Jack Lemmon, Chubby Checker, Isaac Stern, Bob Hope, Peggy Lee, Johnny Mathis, Dana Andrews, Dick Gregory, Liberace, Dizzy Gillespie, the Smothers Brothers, and Andre Kostelanetz; and newsmakers such as astronaut John Glenn, Russian cosmonaut Gherman Titov, Rev. Billy Graham, polio vaccine discoverer Jonas Salk, decathlete and Olympic gold medalist Rafer Johnson, and Walt Disney. There were also major figures-to-be. One was Neil Armstrong, a NASA test pilot who later made history as the first man to walk on the moon. Another was local boy Jim Whittaker, who was about to set

Celebrity fair visitors included George Burns and Carol Channing, who lit her companion's signature cigar with a Needle-inspired lighter.

If the Needle embodied Space Age aspirations, John Glenn embodied its reality. The astronaut, the first American to orbit the earth, visited Century 21. When he saw the Needle, he said, "That's really something." Here at a fair ceremony, with the Needle as backdrop, are (from left) Eddie Carlson, Joe Gandy, Sen. Warren Magnuson, Vice President Lyndon Johnson, Gov. Al Rosellini, Episcopal Bishop William F. Lewis, and Glenn.

off on a major climbing expedition. He returned about a year later as a national hero: the first American to summit Mount Everest.

Security could be inconsistent. John Glenn had to fight crowds on his own on the Observation Deck. A couple of Russian journalists said that the Needle was the only place where they managed to lose their U.S. government minders. And manager Sullivan was once mistakenly roughed up by a U.S. Secret Service agent while trying to welcome the Shah of Iran to the Needle. "This guy had his arm across my throat and his foot on my instep" as he pinned him to the Needle's wall, Sullivan remembered.

All the visitors had varied Needle impressions and opinions, even jokes.

John Wayne toured the fair before its opening with his wife, Pilar, and daughter Aissa: "We were up in the Space Needle last night at sunset. It was just beautiful. Your fair is going to be magnificent."

New York governor Nelson Rockefeller, whose state was preparing to host an expo in 1964-65, made a beeline for the Needle. "This is absolutely fabulous," he said as he scanned the skyline. The elevator ride down was "just like going over Niagara Falls."

Bob Hope came to town to do some shows, and joked about his nose and the Seattle landmark. "I told 'em, 'You certainly picked the right comedian for the fair. What other comic has his own Space Needle?'"

Prince Philip drank gin and tonic and made an amusing remark about the biblical reference in the restaurant's name: "It should give all the rich men of this world new hope and comfort. Now that there is ample room in the Eye of the Needle for any number of camels, they might reasonably expect to make the Kingdom of Heaven when the time comes."

John Glenn, fresh from his trip as the first American to orbit the earth, was most impressed by the Needle, looking up from the ground and exclaiming, "That's really something!"

Alistair Cooke, then a correspondent for England's *Guardian* newspaper and later famed host of *Masterpiece Theatre*, noted that the Needle had been praised widely and described as looking like either "a bow-legged Kewpie doll" or a "Martian's design for a wheatsheaf." He also noted that it gave Seattleites a "godlike view" of their surroundings.

Speaking of god, the Needle also received a visit from a 101-year-old former blacksmith whose only claim to fame was a celebrity name: Isaac Newton. Visiting the top of the Needle, he wryly observed: "This is probably as close to heaven as I'll ever get."

Walt Disney toured the fair as one experienced at creating magic kingdoms. Asked if Disneyland would get a Needle, he said no, but "make no mistake. There will be Space Needles cropping up all over after the success of this one."

As the fair's centerpiece, the Needle was a lightning rod for publicity and promotions. Murray Morgan wrote: "The giant spire was a perfect peg on which news stories could be hung." Not to mention filming movies, showcasing new technologies, and as a platform for stunts—roles that have lasted to this day.

For many, the most enduring image of the Needle during the fair is its association with Elvis Presley. He was a superstar, and Hollywood was churning out multiple Elvis films per year. They decided to shoot one during the fair in Seattle, which was released in 1963 as *It Happened at the World's Fair*. Elvis drew huge crowds when he came to the fair in September of '62, but the Needle was the tallest cast member. Albert Fisher, a twentysomething in charge of television and movies for the fair, was the staffer responsible for

Visitors could pick up a guide to the Needle for 25 cents to learn all kinds of handy facts, such as that the tower and top house had 3,700 tons of high-test steel in them. Or that the automatic vending machines on the Observation Deck could assemble and cook a fresh hamburger in 15 seconds!

coordinating with the filmmakers. "We knew we wanted the Space Needle to play a prominent role in the movie," he said.

A pivotal romantic sequence in the movie is when Elvis takes a date to dinner at the Eye of the Needle. Joan O'Brien plays a World's Fair nurse who Elvis takes a fancy to, and he tricks her into a date by arranging a minor leg injury so he can receive her ministrations. Near the Needle's base, he hires a young fairgoer (played by Kurt Russell in his first film role) to kick him in the leg. Fisher remembered that when they were filming the scene, Elvis took his first real look at the Needle looming overhead and remarked, "That sure is tall. That's one of the tallest things I've ever seen."

Scenes were also shot of Elvis and O'Brien getting onto the elevator, but the trip up was shot in-studio, though Fisher said they needed to get film footage of the ride, so he and a camera crew shuttled up and down the Needle with the doors off to get the required footage. "We had to sign reams of papers like insurance waivers" in order to do that, Fisher recalled.

In the film, Elvis woos his sweetheart with a song ("I'm Falling in Love Tonight") while the Needle turns. That scene, which captures the Needle dining experience so well, was also shot entirely at MGM's Culver Studios, not at the fair. Fisher remembered that the

Elvis visited the fair to film the movie *It Happened at the World's Fair,* but the Needle also had a starring role. An accurate replica of its restaurant was recreated on a soundstage at MGM so that Elvis could appear to woo his costar, Joan O'Brien, over dinner with a song.

1962 № 08158

Seattle World's Fair
THE SPACE NEEDLE CORPORATION

A ticket used to ride up the Needle. During the fair, the trip was $1. From March to October of '62, 2.65 million people went to the top.

During Century 21, probably the oldest man to visit the Needle was a 101-year-old named Isaac Newton, who quipped, "This is probably as close to heaven as I'll ever get."

logistics of shooting in the restaurant during the fair were impossible. The amount of time and equipment required and the resulting disruption ruled it out.

Fisher had befriended Elvis and had even gone on double dates with him during his stay in Seattle. He was hired by MGM as the film's technical adviser and flew down to Los Angeles, where the moviemakers carefully reconstructed a "pizza pie" wedge section of the Needle restaurant in the studio for the love scene. To get the effect of the Needle turning, the film crew had taken photographs of the 360-degree view from the Observation Deck. They then painted a color backdrop of the city skyline at twilight on a revolving drum that rotated in the background to give the impression that the restaurant was turning. It was the opposite of reality—rotating scenery instead of diners—but thanks to relativity, it looked right.

There were various other Needle stunts at the fair. At the opening, Circus Berlin acrobats traversed a wire slung from Memorial Stadium to the 375-foot level of the Needle by motorcycle. Another time, with the aid of fair originator Al Rochester and a former *Playboy*

The Needle was a magnet for stunts. At the opening of the fair, acrobats from Circus Berlin attached a wire from Memorial Stadium to the 375-foot level of the Needle and rode it with a motorcycle.

Playmate, and fueled by loads of free champagne, the press covered the release of a flock of carrier pigeons from the Needle. Some of the pigeons were named after local reporters and their girlfriends. The birds were supposed to carry messages back to the Midwest, but upon release, instead of heading east, they circled the Needle and flew south toward the local pigeon haven of Pioneer Square, much to the amusement of those covering the story. One fair visitor who had wandered in and had five glasses of champagne asked hopefully if this event happened at the Needle *every* morning.

Another legendary stunt was the plan to drop a baseball from the top of the Needle, to be caught by a 19-year-old truck driver from Coney Island, New York, named Sal Durante.

Durante had become a famous fan in the fall of 1961 for catching New York Yankee Roger Maris's record-setting 61st home run. The fair brought Durante to Seattle to show his fielding skills and win a prize of $1,000 if he caught the Needle fastball. Fortunately, a University of Washington physicist pointed out ahead of time that a ball falling from that height would be going 130 mph and could be a lethal beanball, so the promotion was moved to a much lower Ferris wheel on the Gayway. The ball was dropped by pitcher Tracy Stallard, the player who had served up the home run ball to Maris. Stallard had been demoted to the minors and was now in town playing for the Seattle Rainiers. Durante caught five practice catches with style, but dropped the moneyball. As in "Casey at the Bat," the muffed catch produced a loud moan from the crowd. "He did o.k. until we dropped the greased one," joked Jay Rockey, who had orchestrated the stunt. Durante was paid anyway, and sent back home on the first train to New York. The promotion was a bust but is still remembered, even by some who swear the ball was dropped from the Needle.

The Needle faced a few other challenges during the fair. Weather was one, especially the wind. One headache was the natural gas torch on top. The heat from the flames fatigued the metal tower, and there was also trouble screening the wind, which was too often blowing out the torch. Mid-fair, it was shut down for a month for repairs and modified, but it always proved problematic. It was eventually removed, but for those who saw it lit during the Needle's early years, the giant flame on top left an indelible image. When it was relit during the fair, a newspaper captioned a photo: "Shish kebab anyone?"

The Needle elevators would sometimes get stuck. The wind had challenged ironworkers during construction, and now it sometimes played havoc with guests and staff going up and down. A windstorm in late April shut the Needle when the wind gauges registered 70-mph gusts and the night manager, Phil Ireland, got stuck in an elevator and had to walk

One Needle stunt that had to be dropped: tossing a baseball from the Observation Deck to Sal Durante, the young fan who had caught New York Yankee Roger Maris's record home run. It was determined that the ball might kill or injure someone from that height, so the drop was moved to a nearby Ferris wheel on the fair's Gayway.

You knew the Needle had arrived when it became a Jim Beam whiskey decanter in '62.

down. Saying the Needle was built like a strong, flexible reed, the *Times* described what it felt and sounded like upstairs: "The movement atop the Needle was like that of being on a large ship at sea—and not in a storm. The wind blowing through and around the Needle made a noise like a great organ note." The storm passed, and the Needle was open in time for dinner.

An even bigger test came near the end of the fair. On October 12, Seattle was hit with the so-called Columbus Day Storm. The headline in the *P-I*: "32 Dead as Raging Storm Hits NW." It was "the most powerful extratropical cyclone during the past century," University of Washington meteorologist Cliff Mass has written. It hit Seattle at 7:30 p.m. with gusts of 85 mph recorded off West Point. On the Washington coast, winds were clocked at up to 121 mph, and a wind gauge off the Oregon coast broke after registering 145. Broadcast towers were felled in Portland. A Needle elevator got stuck at the 200-foot level with two employees inside, Robert Harvey and Duff Andrews. They passed the time playing rummy, while the winds groaned and shook their shelter, until they were rescued. Needle guests were evacuated by the other working elevators. Seattle radio personality Jim French and his wife were among them. He remembered that as they walked to the fair exit, a big neon sign blew down and crashed at their feet. Still, the Needle passed its first major real-world wind-tunnel test with flying colors.

During the fair, every first-time experience for the Needle got some attention. That summer, even fog made headlines. "Fog Shuts Out View for Needle Breakfasters," one read when the Needle top was fogbound one morning. Another: "Fog Clouds View from Needle." Here's the breathless report: "The 'saucer' on the Space Needle played hide-and-seek in low-lying clouds this morning. Determined spectators strove hard to peer through the gray-white shroud surrounding it. Some got a glimpse of Seattle. Some didn't. Breakfasters who ascended at 7:45 reported 'ceiling zero' the whole time up there. They dawdled over berries and scrambled eggs waiting for the misty curtain to break." Such an "event" would hardly be noticed today, but in 1962, when it came to the Needle, even morning clouds were news.

Although the builders had decided that the Needle would not be a TV broadcast tower like its counterpart in Stuttgart, it still played an interesting and historic role in broadcasting and telecommunications. The Needle featured some of the first wireless telephones, and it became a showcase for emerging global communications technology.

The Needle's connection to the Space Age was sealed with two events in July. The world's first communications satellite, *Telstar 1*, was launched into orbit on July 10. It was built by Bell Labs and owned by AT&T. That evening, the first telephone call transmitted by satellite from Seattle was made from the Space Needle to Washington, D.C. Century 21's general manager, Ewen Dingwall, and Washington governor Albert D. Rosellini talked for just over six minutes with Senator Magnuson on the new hookup. Dingwall said that Magnuson sounded as if he were at the foot of the Needle. Their conversation was broadcast to fairgoers over the public-address system.

Later that month, on July 23, the Needle participated in the first-ever live public trans-Atlantic TV broadcast. The U.S. TV networks set up cameras around the country to transmit images of America to Europe in real time, including President Kennedy and Mount Rushmore. Cameras were set up by KING-TV around the fair grounds, including one at the Eye of the Needle. The fair got about 85 seconds of a 15-minute broadcast at noon, one of the longest segments. The TV audience was estimated at 200 million. The event showed Seattle and the Needle to the world. Albert Fisher credits *Telstar* with everything we take for granted today, from satellite TV to cell phones to wireless Internet. That capability was pioneered by this one satellite, developed and owned by private industry. The Needle had helped demonstrate pioneering technologies, ones we take for granted today.

As the fair began to wrap up, the Needle kept going. It was a permanent new feature and would have a life span far beyond a six-month exhibition. It had been a hit that exceeded anything its builders imagined. Bagley Wright said they collected so much cash during the fair that once a bag containing $5,000 of the day's receipts was misplaced for several days, and no one missed it!

A number of technological firsts took place on the Needle. On July 10, 1962, the first satellite telephone call from Seattle was made thanks to the new *Telstar I* communications satellite, shown here in model form. On the line talking to Senator Magnuson in Washington, D.C., were world's fair general manager Ewen Dingwall and Governor Rosellini.

The original cost of the Needle had been projected at $2.5 million, and by the end of the fair it was $4.3 million, including all the overtime required to handle the unexpected crowds. But it was well into the black. With the private investment already paying off, the question that loomed was, What would they do for an encore? Would the Needle become the "white elephant" some feared? With its iconic status established worldwide, and with a bustling dining room and millions of people who, indeed, were willing to pay $1 for the view, the Needle's owners and Western Hotels managers were optimistic.

Projected Needle attendance had been guesstimated at 1.65 million over six months. But the Needle had hit its 1 millionth visitor by the first of July, when the fair still had nearly four months to run. The final total attendance number, according to Hoge Sullivan, was 2.65 million—an astonishing average of over 12,400 per day. The peak day was August 8, with an astounding 19,300 visitors. The restaurant hosted nearly 470,000, or 2,200 per day. At the end of the fair, Sullivan predicted a total of 3 million visitors by the end of 1962.

The 1,000,000th and 1,000,001st visitors were Mr. and Mrs. Jack Gruber, from Lewiston, Idaho. Gruber remembered waiting in line on July 1, a blustery day. It started to rain and the crowd ran for cover. When it let up, he got back in line ahead of where he would have been before the squall, and he bought the lucky tickets. There was a small ceremony, and he and his wife were escorted to the top of the Needle. Newspaper photographers snapped pictures while the couple was served some impromptu cake and visitors asked for autographs. Later in the day, Jack Gruber remembered, he tried to parlay his celebrity into a free beer at a nearby café. "Sir," said the waitress, "if I gave free beers to everyone who claims to be a celebrity, I wouldn't have a job." The thing that impressed him most, however, was that his sister and brother-in-law were vacationing in the Bahamas and read about him in the local papers there. It said something about the Needle's celebrity, he thought, that this would be news around the world.

The fair closed on October 21, 1962. For the closing ceremonies, a musical and fireworks extravaganza was held at Memorial Stadium that evening, featuring giant fireworks that included one in the shape of an 80-foot-tall Needle. Later that night, the fair attractions began to turn out their lights. The Needle went dark, save for its aircraft warning beacons, and at midnight, the carillon played "Auld Lang Syne." The *Times* described the scene as the lights dimmed: "A misty cloud wrapped the Space Needle, almost hiding it against the night sky. It was almost as if it never happened. Seattle was waking up from a dream. But this dream came true."

Murray Morgan wrote that the "Space Needle marked the turning point" of the world's fair. Now, the Needle had reached its own turning point. It was closed to the public for the next four days to prepare itself for the reentry into the 20th century.

The lighting of the fair and Needle at night were part of creating a dramatic impression. The Needle torch burned brightly, a fiery complement to the night lighting of the fair's International Fountain.

CHAPTER 6

Streakers, Waterbeds, and Controversy

"Through rain, snow, sleet and strikers, the Space Needle carries on."

— Space Needle advertisement

As the fair ended, Seattle congratulated itself and embraced the Needle as a permanent symbol of life after Century 21, as captured in this *Seattle Times* cartoon.

After a miraculous inception and a six-month birth celebration steeped in 21st-century dreams, the now-famous Space Needle reentered the everyday life of the old 20th century in late October 1962. The Space Age fair had been a launchpad for the future, but after Century 21 there were nearly 40 years to go before the actual 21st century arrived. So the Needle would grow up in the decades that it was meant, symbolically, to leapfrog.

Born and christened at the end of the baby-boomer era, the Needle in the ensuing decades has been remarkable in several respects. First is the fact that the patterns for using the Needle have remained consistent over time. It continues to be the place for big stunts and civic events, as well as the dining spot of celebrating families and kings (after Elvis, King Olav of Norway, for one, who said of the view *Dette var flotte* — "That was impressive"). It became the embodiment of the city's public brand, but it also appealed to enduring emotions and reflected cultural trends.

The Needle featured waterbeds and streakers in the '70s, experienced a controversial makeover in the '80s, then became a bit more sober, and the subject of dark humor, at the turn of the millennium. It has been a billboard for movies, seafood, and international events like the Goodwill Games; it has hosted exhibits of science-fiction memorabilia and Bigfoot and became the storybook home of the Wheedle. It has embraced the fashions and symbolism of its times. Its mod tangerine-colored top house gave way to more neutral whites and golds. Elvis crooned there during the fair, the Beatles talked about it in the '60s, Kurt Cobain hung out there in the '90s. The Needle became a screen on which the panorama of life and culture in Seattle has been projected for a half-century.

And during those years, the Needle was tested too. Each decade brought challenges and debates. There were earthquakes, alarms (false) raised about the Needle's collapse, scares over terrorism, and major disagreements about whether the Needle should serve public or private interests, or both. If the Needle came into being after a surprisingly short gestational period, it has continued to grow in and on Seattle, shaped by the times and experience.

Opposite Page
The steel Needle contrasted with other colorful Space Age totems, these "carved" by machine for the fair's South Gate and designed by Bassetti & Morse.

The World's Highest DJ, a Big Quake, and UFO Skywatchers

In some respects, the Needle's postfair transition was easy. The model worked as a business and attraction: tens of thousands came to ride, look, and dine. The biggest change was the volume. In the years following the fair, the Needle has averaged roughly one million visitors annually, strong attendance, though nothing like the fair's frenzy. The skyline changed, but not much else. The menu was high-end, the wait staff dressed in colorful uniforms (one 1960s critic referred to the waitresses as "space maidens swathed in American-Voluptuary gold lamé"), the restaurant still turned, and locals came up for a treat.

In 1963, the first marriage on the Needle took place. William Lyon, age 23, and his bride, Sunnye Rushing, 20, were wed on the Observation Deck on January 18. The couple, both Boeing employees, celebrated with cake, steak, and champagne. Other couples eyed the Needle as a potential love nest. Later that year, a would-be bride from Connecticut wrote to the Needle saying that she and her fiancé were looking for a future home and asked if the Needle was available, and if so, at what price?

The city changed too. In contrast with the fair, trees along the Monorail route made it seem like truly green transportation.

Another guest was a young Bill Gates, who in 1966 won a dinner at the Needle from his church pastor for memorizing the Sermon on the Mount. Not everyone visited the Needle, but they noticed it. When Seattle was gripped by Beatlemania in 1964, the Fab Four were asked about the Needle in a preconcert interview at the Seattle Center Coliseum:

Unknown Reporter: "Did you see the Needle at all, Paul?"

Paul: "Yeah, the Space Needle."

Unknown Reporter: "Did you go up?"

Paul: "No. (crowd laughs) But I saw it."

George: "It looks better from the ground."

John: "I don't like heights."

To some extent, the Needle would go the way of Seattle Center. The more Seattle Center generated a dynamic or fairlike atmosphere, the better. The Needle owners and staff wanted the Monorail to keep running because it delivered so many visitors to the Needle's base. With the fair over, visitors could also find nearby parking.

But there was change in the wind. The Needle was never a broadcast tower like Stuttgart's, but it was a great platform for broadcasters. In 1963, in cooperation with KING Broadcasting, a glassed-in radio booth was built on the east side of the Observation Deck facing the Cascades, Capitol Hill, and the new I-5 freeway. According to the papers, it was "the world's highest radio studio." KING ensconced its morning radio DJ Frosty Fowler there to broadcast his 6-10 a.m., six-day-a-week music and chat program, and it was the number-

The Needle lived on in the '60s and '70s, and adjusted its marketing to reflect the times.

one show in Seattle. The Eye of the Needle restaurant had been more prosaically renamed the Space Needle Restaurant, but there was now an eye in the sky watching over the town. Alfred Frankenstein, a San Francisco columnist, had spotted the Needle's potential along this line almost immediately. In 1962 he wrote, "Big Brother could easily use the top platform of the Needle to keep the whole Northwest under surveillance."

Fowler immediately understood the power of the Needle as both a prop and a platform. He climbed the Needle's mast, he went outside and hung from the painter's scaffold (and got stuck), he used his perch to tease and titillate the city. He'd peer into the Edgewater Inn's parking lot with his telescope to report on local license plates of cars parked there for, the implication being, naughty behavior. Such ideas ran as a theme through many Seattleites' thoughts: What could you see from up there, peeping into Seattle's apartments and penthouses?

The post-fair Needle evolved its festive offerings, from tiki cocktails to tropical fruits, to keep its international flavor.

The Needle continued to be a draw for fine dining. Some critics compared the experience to going on a cruise.

During the fair, a local folk duo, Mike and Maggie Moloso, performed and recorded a spoof song at the Pioneer Square folk club 92 Yesler. It was called "Wasn't That a Mighty Day When the Needle Hit the Ground," telling the tale of a group of voyeuristic Needle visitors who rush to peer into a woman's boudoir and thus tip the Needle over. Fowler used to pretend that he could see into the dressing room of a woman who coordinated a fashion show at the Space Needle for KING-TV and would advise her on the air about what to wear. She was furious until she realized it was a joke.

Fowler, who sometimes breakfasted on steak, fiddlehead ferns, and a "glass of white foaming something" from the Needle restaurant to get him going, was jokingly called "the world's highest disc jockey." In 1964, he participated in an around-the-world goodwill

Space Needle Gift Shops, Seattle, U.S.A.

The souvenir shop on the Observation Deck continued to do a brisk business even after the fair.

WASN'T THAT A MIGHTY DAY
WHEN THE NEEDLE HIT THE GROUND
and THE THREE RAVENS

Mike & Maggie

A LIVE RECORDING IN SEATTLE'S HOTTEST NEW BASEMENT BISTRO

. . . featuring

THE COUNTRY'S MOST EXCITING NEW FOLK MUSIC TEAM, MIKE AND MAGGIE

92 YESLER

PHOTO / BOB PETERSON

RECORDED AT 92 YESLER WAY, SEATTLE, WASHINGTON   Price $1.25

The Needle entered folk culture with "Wasn't That a Mighty Day When the Needle Hit the Ground," a spoof song that imagined what would happen if the Needle fell over: "Well, the restaurant kept rolling/right on down Denny Way./It cut the Viaduct in half/and it landed in the Bay."

tour with the Needle's manager, Hoge Sullivan, and Miss Space Needle, Judy Saunders, visiting all the major tower restaurants, from the Eiffel Tower to towers in Tokyo, Stuttgart, Cairo, and Frankfurt, and filing radio reports along the way.

A Fowler absence for a different reason marked a celebrity moment for the Needle. In the fall of 1963, Fowler was injured in a traffic accident. KING hustled to find a substitute host. A young up-and-coming comedian was in town performing at the Opera House, and was tapped to fill in while Fowler recuperated. That's how Bill Cosby became a Needle broadcaster for the better part of a week that November. "I've enjoyed every minute of it," Cosby told the *Seattle Times*. "But getting down to the station at 5 a.m. is murder." Cosby introduced a character, "Dr. Ybsoc" (Cosby backwards), who gave expert advice on everything, such as suggesting that city buses put perfume in their diesel fuel to improve the aroma.

Fowler was on the air during the Needle's first major seismic test. The structural engineers were concerned about wind and earthquakes. The Needle had already passed a real-world wind test during the unprecedented Columbus Day cyclone of '62. At 8:29 a.m. on April 29, 1965, a magnitude 6.5 earthquake hit the region. Fowler was playing a Connie Francis record when it struck, and he said the needle on the Needle didn't skip. He went on the air to assure people that the tower and the city were still standing. Still, the strong quake created an I-remember-where-I-was moment for everyone who lived through it, especially those who were high up on the Needle and felt the tower sway back and forth. "It was," said Needle restaurant manager Basil Miaullis, like "riding the top of a flagpole."

Downstairs from Fowler's studio, KING-TV was broadcasting a live morning show, *Telescope*, from the Needle restaurant, which was packed with breakfast diners enjoying various segments, including a fashion show. Sue Albrecht of KING was there. She remembered that the models used a Needle elevator for a dressing room, and could see the ground moving through the slit between the elevator and the floor. "The Needle swayed and you could see the movement from Queen Anne almost to West Seattle," she said. There was no panic, though she remembered "three people demanded that we get them out of the Needle before the broadcast ended, and they were walked slowly down the stairs to the ground." A couple of Space Needle employees were said to have fled, never to return.

Architect John Graham rushed to the Needle to make sure everything was okay and reassure the public. George Schuchart ran into the street outside the Howard S. Wright offices and watched the Needle sway in a slow figure-eight pattern, doing, he said, just what it was designed to do. The Needle has a low center of gravity and was built specifically to withstand serious quakes. It came through with no major damage, save some water sloshed from a fish tank and the loss of a bottle of champagne and a "couple bottles of booze," Miaullis said. "This place was built to take it." Now that had been proved.

In 1966, KING left the Needle and KIRO radio took its place with a beefed-up lineup of shows and features, including a morning show hosted by Jim French. KIRO had DJs throughout the day, plus a ham radio setup and a network of ham operators reporting news from what they called the 'Round the World Amateur Radio Control Center. The station also introduced short-wave radio traffic reports provided by commuters with CB radios. And KIRO-TV installed a TV camera on top of the Needle so it could broadcast live remote images of Seattle during its station ID breaks. Clearly, the view from the Needle was not about peeping *into* the city's bedrooms so much as hosting technology that was allowing Seattleites to keep an eye on the city *from* their bedrooms.

Opposite Page
After the fair, the Needle became a broadcast beacon. It featured a radio studio, a live TV camera on top, and a ham radio setup for getting news from around the world.

A group of UFO "Skywatchers" used to meet at night to search the skies from the Observation Deck, and the Needle's lighting sometimes took on a saucer look.

The mood lighting inside the restaurant made it seem like the most romantic saucer ride imaginable as diners hovered above the city.

The viewing platform also extended to watching the skies. The saucerlike Needle became a perch from which to look for UFOs when KIRO's French organized The Skywatchers, volunteer citizens including believers and skeptics who agreed to spend evenings from 6:00 to midnight scanning the heavens. "As it began to get dark, people in the group would come up the Needle and bring their telescopes and field glasses. It was good for everybody, the people, the listeners. I was very serious about it," said French. He was serious because he had seen UFOs himself. "I knew the phenomenon was real, not someone's imagination." The effort was not successful, however. No UFOs were spotted.

The Needle, however, participated in a citywide effort to make itself visible from space. In July 1969, as *Apollo 11* returned home from its historic landing on the moon, it passed right over the Pacific Northwest as it headed for splashdown in the Pacific. With French broadcasting live from the Needle, all eyes turned heavenward and Seattle, Portland, and Vancouver, B.C., turned their lights on to salute the passing astronauts and welcome them back to earth.

During the 1960s, the Needle experienced other challenges, including a restaurant workers' strike and lockout, as well as inclement weather. In December of 1968 a record deep-freeze closed the Needle when the water pipes froze at 10 degrees. A storm in '69 covered the top house in snow, which melted, then refroze, surrounding the roof with beautiful and potentially deadly icicles. Workers were sent out in the restaurant-level window-washer, and one knocked the icicles down with a hammer while another caught them in a salmon net. After that, the roof was salted. The Needle ran a newspaper ad to reassure guests with an end-of-the-decade message: "Through rain, snow, sleet and strikers, the Space Needle carries on."

For a PONCHO auction in 1974, the Needle donated a lifetime family pass. It was purchased by the auctioneer James G. Murphy for $500. The metal ticket is still honored. It is one of only a few such passes ever issued. Murphy says he's gotten his money's worth.

Ch-Ch-Ch-Changes

The '70s was a weird, tumultuous decade, and no less so for the Needle. The tower turned 10, experienced its first deaths and a birth, entered children's lore, featured a penthouse with a waterbed, rode out the Boeing recession, experienced the energy crisis, and appeared in a film as a symbol of post-Watergate cynicism and malaise. The Needle also experienced an ownership shift and stirred controversy over a proposed addition. For a landmark, the Needle certainly wasn't standing still.

The fair had ended on a high note. Ewen Dingwall, Century 21's general manager and later head of Seattle Center, said, "A whole new generation of civic leaders came into being—exhausted, triumphant, convinced they could accomplish almost anything they set their minds to." But there was a letdown immediately after the fair, with Boeing cutbacks and Seattle Center transitioning from a glamorous fair site to an everyday amenity. In a column in the *San Francisco Chronicle*, writer Neil Morgan wrote of a visit to the Needle in 1963 to check the postfair mood. "From atop the Space Needle . . . the show is better than ever," he wrote. "But, down below . . . much of the site of the fair has gone honky-tonk." He also noted that Seattle storefronts were filled with "vacancy" signs.

As the Needle approached its 10th anniversary in 1972, more Boeing layoffs, the cancellation of the Supersonic Transport program, the loss of the major league Seattle Pilots franchise after a single season, and increased skepticism about booster-driven progress changed the mood of the city. Columnist Rick Anderson, reflecting on the rough-ride decade after the fair, said that people had hoped Century 21 would help Seattle turn the corner. "But halfway through the corner, crash."

It was the era of the billboard "Will the last person leaving Seattle – Turn out the lights," but for its birthday, the Needle was lighting up. A worldwide search was conducted for a genuine lamplighter to come and light 10 giant gas-fed candles fitted on the Needle's roof for the 10th anniversary. They actually hired one of the last gas lamplighters from London, Ivan Ramnauth, to come over and do the job.

The Needle had continued to do well. In 1972, Bagley Wright said, "It hasn't been the great bonanza some people think, but it has returned a good profit." Annual attendance was still steady and strong. But hard reality struck in different forms. In 1973, during the energy crisis, the Needle did its bit to save energy by turning out its lights at night for the first time since the end of the fair. "The switches were pulled on six 1,500-watt bulbs at the base and 24 70-watt fluorescent lights on the roof," it was reported. It was an early sign that the days of unlimited lighting and blazing gas torches were ending. In 1974, Spokane would host the first green-themed international exposition, looking at a future of limited resources.

In the early 1970s, local artists began to play with the question "Is the Space Needle art?" At the forefront was the experimental, nonprofit And/Or gallery on Capitol Hill. Anne

The Space Needle has long attracted the attention of science fiction buffs. Starting in the '70s, a series of sci-fi X-Pos took place at Seattle Center, often with special exhibits at the Needle.

Sci-fi X-Po guests included the two standing in the center of this picture, George Takei, Lt. Sulu from *Star Trek*, and the white-haired movie director Robert Wise, who directed *Star Trek: The Motion Picture*. Both signed autographs at the Needle.

Focke, who staffed the Seattle Arts Commission and was one of the founders of Bumbershoot and Artist Trust, ran the gallery. It was devoted to provocative experimental, conceptual, and performance art.

In 1974, on the Needle's 12th anniversary, an And/Or group calling themselves the Seattle Souvenir Service displayed their "Space Needle Collection," a batch of souvenir items and images of the Needle ranging from large models of the Needle to cigarette lighters, ashtrays, scarves, crystal, photos, postcards, and various other assorted tchotchkes. One mysterious postal art item was titled "Horny Space Needle Emerging from Mississippi River in Response to the Mating Call of the Gateway Arch." The collection of 350 objects were soberly cataloged and displayed. The purpose, said Focke, was to "take art off its pedestal." The catalog featured images of the Needle that popped up around town in backyards and along busy commercial streets as a kind of folk art, including one that had been built from "'keen junk,' leftover paint, and a barbecue motor" by two guys in Edmonds. At the very least, the Needle has inspired folk art.

Tragedy struck unexpectedly in 1974. On March 4, a slender, bearded, redheaded young man named Paul Baker bummed the money to ride to the Observation Deck, jumped over the glass barrier, and became the Needle's first suicide. For a tower born in optimism, built without a single fatality, the suicide seemed a tragic anomaly. There were two more suicides, the last in 1978. The Needle took strong steps to stop them. Today, the Observation Deck is enclosed with a cable mesh "space cage" for safety.

In 1974, Hollywood released Alan J. Pakula's thriller *The Parallax View* starring Warren Beatty, about a reporter on the trail of a conspiracy that begins with a political assassination on the Needle's Observation Deck. Critic William Arnold in the *Seattle P-I* noted a major shift. The architecture of optimism of the '60s was now seen in the Watergate era as representing darker political forces. "The Space Needle," he wrote, "framed ominously in the opening shots of the film, becomes the supreme symbol for this dehumanization. . . ."

But for others, the Needle represented thrill-seeking, not gloom. In 1975, two men, Ken Gorman and Ron Herman, smuggled parachutes to the Observation Deck. They used tools to remove the glass and metal barriers and slipped onto the halo. They then jumped, shocking diners in the restaurant as they zipped past as their chutes opened. On the ground, the two tried to sell their story and photos to the local papers for $500. It turned out there was no specific law against what they did, but they were charged with reckless endangerment. They were found "not guilty," however, by Judge Barbara Yanick, who said that while what they did was "foolhardy," it did not represent a substantial risk to anyone but themselves.

The Needle was not immune to the '70s streaking craze. If diners were shocked by dropping parachutists, they got an even better view of a naked man hanging out the door of a small plane that circled the Needle in June 1974. UPI reported, "A nude man dangled

from the door of a small airplane that twice circled the 607-foot symbol of the 1962 World's Fair." Some patrons dropped their utensils, while others applauded. One witness, Don McDaniel, said, "He was tan. He was just waving his arms and legs." The main law broken was by the pilot: planes were supposed to maintain a horizontal distance of 2,000 feet away from the Needle. In March 1975 another streaker struck. A diner in the restaurant stripped off his clothes, ran around the dining room, then plopped back down in his seat. He was arrested and booked for lewdness. Apparently, he had no escape plan.

Streaking wasn't the only goofy stunt at the top of the Needle. KING and KIRO were long gone, but Seattle's country music station, KAYO, put one of their popular DJs, "Bashful" Bobby Wooten, on the Needle from October 1974 to April 1975 as part of a joint promotional effort. Wooten didn't just occupy a broadcast booth. At a cost of $50,000, a complete 1,200-square-foot penthouse was constructed. It featured a living room, bathroom with tub, and octagonal waterbed. The pad was decorated with Indian art, wood paneling, and, it being the '70s, white shag carpeting throughout. Plus, Wooten's wife Patty lived there with him. The penthouse was open to public viewing during Needle hours. Listeners were invited to submit names for the apartment, and they included "Cute Woot's Hi-Falute," "The Celestial Outhouse," "1150 Wooten Towers," "The Star Spangled Manor," and "Flyin' Wootenanny."

KAYO, formerly a rock station of the "Twist" era, was now devoted to keeping Seattle from getting too big for its big-city britches. Not long after the fair, the station took a cow named Miss Carnation Sally Lola Princess up the Needle for milking. "She was real good—didn't have an accident 'til on the way down," a KAYO spokesman said. One of the station's legendary DJs, Buck Ritchey, ran a spoof campaign for mayor. Among his proposals was turning the Needle's torch into a windmill water pump that would "fill every trough in six counties. No cow in Seattle would go thirsty." The Needle may have aspired to Eiffel Tower elegance, but it wasn't above pure cornpone.

Two births occurred at the Needle in 1974. One was a premature baby born on the mezzanine level to a visitor from Denver. The other was the Wheedle. In 1974, children's author Stephen Cosgrove wrote and published *Wheedle on the Needle*, the tale of a furry orange Bigfoot-like creature with a bright red nose who finds a home on top of the Needle: "There's a Wheedle on the Needle/I know just what you're thinking/But if you look up late at night/You'll see his red nose blinking." The book is still in print, and the Wheedle for a time was a ubiquitous character in Seattle pop culture, including a stint in the '80s as the official mascot for the Seattle SuperSonics basketball team.

He wasn't the only strange character to show up at the Needle. In 1977, Marvel published a comic book featuring an angry Godzilla ravaging Seattle and attacking the Needle, munching on it as if it were a Dick's Deluxe burger. No mention of what happened to the Wheedle during the attack.

Bobby's Space Needle Penthouse

Bashful Bobby Wooten, Kountry KAYO's morning man, has been broadcasting and living high in Seattle's Space Needle. Bobby and his wife Patty Mae live in a one-bedroom penthouse, 520 feet up, on the Observation Deck.

The living area is right out of our Northwest.
The apartment is full of the Northwest with driftwood, greens of the forest, burnt oranges, and sculpture by area artists. Interior design by Bernard Mankertz of Seattle.

Space Age Country kitchen.
Walk into Patty Mae's kitchen and get ready for some down-home Country cooking. The kitchen's a gourmet's delight with authentic Northwest Indian carvings.

Bobby's 'birthday' bath.
And, when you want to take a dip, dive into Bobby's 'birthday' bath tub! The bathroom has a back wall of genuine Northwest barn wood. And an antique deer head for holding your towel while you bathe.

In 1974-75, "Bashful" Bobby Wooten, a country music DJ from KAYO radio, occupied a custom-built penthouse on the Needle with all the '70s amenities, including shag carpet and an octagonal waterbed.

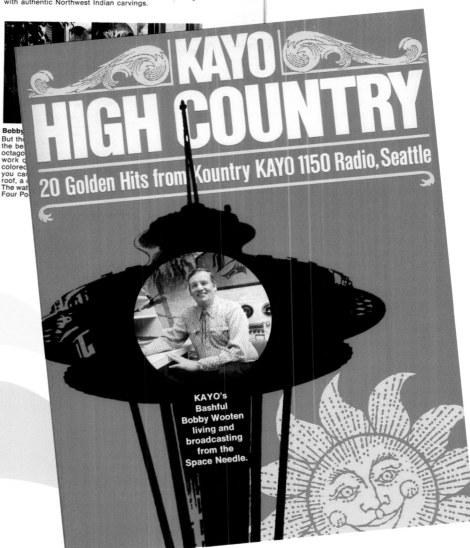

KAYO
HIGH COUNTRY
20 Golden Hits from Kountry KAYO 1150 Radio, Seattle

KAYO's Bashful Bobby Wooten living and broadcasting from the Space Needle.

In 1978, the Observation Deck hosted a Sasquatch exhibit. And starting in the late 1970s on into the '80s, the Needle would turn its top into a flying saucer with special lighting and host events tied in with the annual sci-fi expo at Seattle Center. Needle guests included Boomer of *Battlestar Galactica*, the original Buck Rogers actor Buster Crabbe, Hollywood animator George Pal, sci-fi/fantasy artist William Stout, *Star Trek*'s Sulu, and famed science fiction author Poul Anderson.

The decade also saw some major changes at the Needle. One was a shift in ownership in 1976. The Howard S. Wright family bought out three of the original Needle investors, Bagley Wright, Ned Skinner, and Norton Clapp. Bagley Wright later said that he had hoped Pentagram would become a major force in local development, and the company did do the Bank of California Center downtown. But over time, the partners' interests diverged, and the Wright-Schuchart family, partners in the construction business and the Needle investment, expanded their stake. Architect John Graham also remained an owner, though he later left the partnership too. The original investors had done well, but now the Needle was mostly in the hands of one family. Chairman Jeff Wright described his father, Howard, as being on a "burning quest to maintain his ownership" of the Needle and rising to the challenges of keeping it thriving.

In 1978, the Needle's management let it be known that they were planning on adding a new $1 million restaurant at the 100-foot level of the Space Needle. It would also feature a lounge and dance floor. Their hope was to build it in time for the Seattle Art Museum's King Tut exhibit, slated to open that July at Seattle Center. They anticipated little trouble. After all, the Needle itself had been built in little more than a year. The original John Graham & Co. design imagined view levels at the intermediate platforms of the tower. However, the new design of what became known as the Skyline Level extended beyond the tripod tower. Because the original permit for the Needle, a structure that didn't conform to city code, had been issued by the City Council, it was decided that the council had to approve any major changes.

What resulted was a struggle between the Needle and opponents of the Skyline restaurant plan. The Needle argued that changing times and increasing maintenance costs required that they look for new ways to generate revenue. Opponents, led by Victor Steinbrueck, Allied Arts, and a neighborhood group headed by preservationist Art Skolnik, United South Slope Residents of Queen Anne Hill, argued that the project tampered with what was in effect a local landmark and ruined its architectural integrity.

Between the City Council and the Needle, there was an argument over principle. Did the council, in fact, have the right to approve or disapprove the permit, and if so, on what basis? Was the Needle a privately owned landmark that ought to be subject to more control by the city? Or was it a privately owned facility with the same rights as other businesses? As Walt Crowley wrote in 1979, "The Space Needle became a symbol of a new sort, the symbol of a contest between public and private rights in the arena of development."

The shy Wheedle emerged in 1974, a Bigfoot-type creature that lived on the Needle. Its red nose (pinched here by a young girl in the University District) could be seen blinking at night. The popular children's story character went on to become a mascot for the Seattle SuperSonics.

The Needle has also attracted critters. In 1977, Marvel comics dispatched Godzilla to show Seattle how to transform a waterfront, and how to turn the Needle into a Dick's Deluxe hamburger.

In October 1978, the City Council voted down the new restaurant addition. The Needle owners decided to contest the action in court. Seeing an opportunity amid discord, a group of business leaders in the city of Fife announced they would pay the Needle owners $1 million to move the tower there, where they would find a more sympathetic civic environment.

The council debate pushed the project back so that there was no possibility of building it in time for King Tut. Even so, the Tut show was a smash, with nearly 1.3 million attendees during the four-month exhibit, a boon for the Seattle Art Museum, Seattle Center, and the Needle, which saw its largest attendance since the world's fair: 1.4 million people went

to the top in '78. Visitors were tempted by Tut souvenirs, a Tut menu, even the "Tut Tut" cocktail of cranberry liqueur and fruit juices. That year's Needle attendance figure has not since been surpassed.

More good news for the Needle owners came in 1979, when Superior Court Judge Francis Holman said that the City Council could not, in fact, decline the Needle's permit for essentially aesthetic reasons. The Needle was too young to be an official landmark. The only valid basis for turning the permit down or adding new requirements would be to protect "life, property or public welfare," but the city Building Department had already said that the Needle plans met safety requirements. Still, the City Council appealed the decision, kicking it back into court. Supporters of the project on the council were upset. The *Times* quoted Councilmember John Miller: "'It offends my sense of fairness' to deny the permit on that [aesthetic] basis alone, he said. 'The fact that they (owners of the Needle) are wealthy doesn't mean they aren't entitled to fairness.'" A *Times* editorial criticized Seattle's "endless debate" on the topic and quoted the paper's own columnist John Hinterberger in calling the dispute the "babble of tower."

A final decision would come in the next decade.

Opposite Page
As the Needle closed the '70s, it had become a skyline fixture, but with the world's fair a decade and a half behind it, some changes were coming.

CHAPTER 7

"Grunge, Coffee, and the Space Needle"

"Unless the Space Needle falls down, don't call me."

— John Keister quoting a Seattle media saying

Not all reviews of the Space Needle over the years have been positive. Even the Eiffel Tower outraged some Parisians. The writer Guy de Maupassant called the Paris landmark a "horrid nightmare" and said he ate there frequently so that he wouldn't have to look at it.

In 1962, at a confab of architects convened at Century 21, Warnett Kennedy, the town-planning director of the Architectural Institute of British Columbia, dismissed the Needle as "a beautiful example of gimmicktecture" and jokingly imagined a future of restaurants in diving bells and balloons. Writing about the fair in May 1962 for *Saturday Review*, art critic Katharine Kuh judged the Needle "a monstrosity." She went on: "Designed by local architects, this pretentious and vulgar structure (sad when compared to the Eiffel Tower) does irreparable damage to the grandeur of Seattle's natural setting."

Even in more recent times, some have seen the Needle as modern kitsch. Seattle writer Jonathan Raban, a British expat, wrote in a 1993 essay, "Living with the Space Needle on the other side of Queen Anne Hill was rather like having to put up with a black-velvet portrait of Jesus on one's living room wall." He did decide that the Needle had a message to deliver, not about the Space Age but Seattle's own ambitions. It was a symbol of "Seattle's capital status across the hinterland" of the Great Northwest. It is certainly true that the Needle had local, regional, national, and international messages to send, and claiming regional ascendancy was one of them.

George Ross Leighton, who had written a series of articles for *Harper's* on world's fairs, was taken by the Needle and recognized it as a powerful legacy for the cityscape. He covered Century 21 for a history of international expositions he was writing, and he was impressed, colors and all. "The Needle has been described as 'sheaf shaped' and that is so, but in some respects it suggests a flower. The graceful off-white enamel of its legs soar up and burst into flame color at the crown and the effect on a bright day is enchanting. What would the Paris skyline be today without Eiffel's masterpiece? It is not too early to say: Where would the skyline of Seattle be today without the Space Needle?"

Where, indeed. That skyline has changed dramatically over the years. The Needle remained the tallest building in town until 1969, with the completion of the black-box skyscraper called then the Seattle-First National Bank building on Fourth Avenue downtown. It was immediately dubbed "The box the Space Needle came in," and in the days when the two towers were the city's tallest structures, standing roughly in line with one another, their proportions suggested a Jim Beam decanter and its gift box. Other buildings have since topped the Needle, notably the 76-story Columbia Center, whose developer, Martin Selig, claimed to have bribed his way to the top of the Needle as a young man during its construction by giving Space Needle T-shirts to the entire crew.

Was the Needle a masterpiece, or an eyesore? Was it historic, or a gimmick? As time went on, critics weighed in on what it meant to the city.

Despite growth and taller towers, the Needle has maintained its identity. As Seattle grew up, the Needle's unique look and location became even more critical: It did not get lost in a forest of high-rises; it stood apart with a style all its own, just as the Eiffel Tower stands tall in low-rise Paris. Rob Carson in *Pacific Northwest* magazine in 1987 wrote, "The Space Needle soars high above blissful in its passé splendor, forever unfailing as a point of reference."

One strange example of the Needle's stature as a reference point: In 1984, two prison inmates in San Francisco "confessed" to being responsible for the Green River serial killings in an ill-considered scheme to effect an escape. Detectives figured out they were lying when one of the inmates "couldn't describe the Space Needle." Familiarity with the landmark was now defining in terms of identity.

A proposed restaurant addition stirred civic debate. Jeanne Beall and Jim Going, representing the Needle and its architects, wooed media support by serenading *Seattle Post-Intelligencer* writer John O'Ryan during an open-air lunch on the 100-foot level.

Essential to the City's "Psychological Well-Being"

The Skyline restaurant debate was a key moment in determining what the Needle was, and how important it was to the community. John Hinterberger outlined two sides of the aesthetic debate: "There are those in this city who believe fervently that the Space Needle is a piece of architectural poetry and that to embellish any of its lines is a travesty to art and form and society. There are others to whom it is a leggy novelty, a leftover curiosity from a lesser exposition and a fair model for a paperweight." Was it art, junk, or something in between?

The Needle responded to Skyline critics with a PR campaign that included wining and dining a newspaper columnist on the 100-foot-level platform. There was also an ad showing a model of the Needle with its addition, which looked far sleeker and much less intrusive than some of its cartooning critics had implied by sketching an addition that resembled a hamburger. The burger accusation was bogus. "If we thought the new facility at the Space Needle would look like a hamburger on a T-shirt—we'd be upset too," the owners said. John Graham & Co. argued that they had designed the original Needle, and knew what they were doing. Certainly Graham and the original investors wanted the Needle to be both a commercial success and an inspiring landmark.

One novel argument regarding the Skyline addition was offered by the University of Washington's James Wise, an associate professor of architecture and psychology. He thought changing the Needle could be unduly stressful for locals. He said that citizens needed

During construction, people could get a good view of the outriggers that support the Skyline Level. They echo the structure of the sunburst of beams underneath the top house.

"environmental anchors" like the Needle for "psychological well-being." Wise said, "The higher the symbolic content, as with something like the Space Needle, the more important it is to leave it alone." In other words, don't tamper with the totem. Wise's concerns took as fact that the Needle was now an essential symbolic fixture in the city's ecosystem.

In 1981, the Needle won when the court of appeals found that the City Council had erred by not having officially and explicitly declared its findings and conclusions in denying the Skyline permit in 1978. The city decided not to appeal, so the project went ahead. The dispute established that the Needle owners could modify their property as private owners; aesthetics were not a legitimate basis for denying a permit. The furor also served as a reminder that the Needle walked a tricky tightrope. The tower had been developed by risk-taking private investors, but it also flourished in part because of public investment in Seattle Center. Some of that tension and need for balance is embodied in the Needle's design, with its wide top set upon a narrow base of gravity-defying curved girders and upheld by fingers of steel. Its solid foundation consists of concrete, steel, and vast public goodwill.

In the meantime, things had changed in three years. Instead of $1 million, the cost of the Skyline addition had nearly doubled to $1.7 million. Instead of a full-scale restaurant, it would now host a smaller café, kitchen facilities, and room for special events. It wasn't finished until mid-1982, more than four years after it was proposed. Apparently, the era of 400-day wonders was over.

It did change the profile of the Needle, but from a distance, it hardly seemed to make a difference. Still, the Needle had become an unofficial landmark, and some people didn't want it to change.

The so-called Skyline Level facility was designed by John Graham & Co. to handle diners and special events.

An upside of the Skyline controversy was that the city was on record as considering the Needle to be an important landmark. After a mere 20 years, it was solidly set in the city's psyche. It not only told the world where Seattle was, but also reminded Seattle of who it was. When the Needle officially received city landmark status in 1999, it was the city's youngest. It was also the first to meet all six of the city's landmark criteria. In historic-preservation terms, that was the equivalent of a grand slam.

As the city grew, Seattleites expressed a feeling of protectiveness toward the Needle. Many homes and apartments were sold offering Space Needle views, and people complained when those were blocked by new development. A 1963 ad for the new Maison Ville apartments on Capitol Hill promised an "unobstructed view" of "your Eiffel Tower." A 2001 study instigated under Mayor Paul Schell identified public sightlines of the Needle to be preserved for posterity. At least 10, called "beloved views" on the city's website, have been protected by law, including those from Alki Beach, Gas Works Park, Kerry Park, Volunteer Park, and Seattle Center itself. The Needle's landmark ordinance specified that any development next to or across the street from the tower be subject to review for its impact on the Needle.

Today, the Skyline Level is used for events and banquets. Below, the Pavilion, added in 2000, protects guests from the elements and features a gift shop, a reservation desk, and a spiral ramp for visitors to the Skyline Level and Observation Deck.

With the Skyline addition, the Needle had jumped the hurdle to become a structure both beloved and taken seriously by Seattleites. Eddie Carlson's daughter, Jane Carlson Williams, who worked at the Needle during the fair, described her father's reaction to the controversy: "He loved the fact that the citizens had embraced it as our city's symbol, and were saying, 'How dare you change it?' That was very satisfying to him."

Today, the Skyline Level is simply a part of the beloved structure, the essence of which remains intact. The elaborate Pavilion at the base of the Needle, which features the gift shop, the restaurant check-in, and a curving spiral ramp for waiting Observation Deck visitors, is a glassed-in structure partly based on the unbuilt original design for an entrance at the foot of the Needle. It was designed in careful consultation with the landmarks board to maintain the Needle's architectural integrity. It opened in 2000 as part of a major $20 million Needle renovation that also included the new SkyCity restaurant in the top house and a circular entrance drive—essentially a reboot of the Needle for the 21st century. Easements were also obtained for the top house, which extended out over the original property line. It was all done without any of the fuss of the Skyline era, and it helped to complete the original Needle concept. It set the Needle up for the new century by adding and extending features that would help it continue to flourish in the decades ahead. Part of what enabled that was the continued ownership by a family who had not only built the Needle, but also embraced it fully.

The concept for the spiral ramp is shown in this Earle Duff rendering of the Needle. It gives an idea of what John Graham & Co. intended. It also illustrates the concept of having view platforms at the 100- and 200-foot levels.

Over time, the Needle has looked to add features at the lower levels that fulfilled ideas that were part of the earlier design: views from intermediate levels, and a real entrance.

A Makeover, a Giant Crab, and April Fool's

The early 1980s were a time of big change at the Needle. With its 20th anniversary approaching, the Space Needle planned to take over running the restaurant from Westin Hotels as their 20-year lease on the operation ran out. There had been cosmetic changes over the years, but now the restaurant would receive a complete makeover, and in the fall of 1981, the Needle hosted an on-site auction to sell off all the original furniture and fixtures. The Needle would enter its twenties with new independence: consolidated ownership, more control over its operations, a new look, and a new wardrobe to match.

Also, with a more populist attitude. In 1982, the Needle invited the public to come down and up to "see and taste what's new." One motivation was an attempt to appeal more to locals. "We've found that most Seattle people think the Needle is for out-of-towners," said Frank Finneran, who was in charge of the makeover. "We know visitors will come, but we're going to focus more on local trade." Seattle loved the Needle, but it also was important to get them inside it. For years, the Needle had been hosting special events and occasions: Halloween parties, Thanksgiving dinners, Santa breakfasts, New Year's celebrations, even Mardi Gras dances, all ways of boosting use during the off-season months. Now it wanted to provide more options year-round.

The Skyline Level opened for banquets, meetings, and events, but instead of a full-scale restaurant it was home to the family-friendly Wheedle's at the Needle, an inexpensive café serving sandwich fare. You could go up for a bite without paying the elevator fee. The top house restaurant was divided into two dining areas: the 180-seat Space Needle Restaurant, with menu items starting at under $10 and featuring Northwest foods under the heading "Cuisine of the Public Market," and a smaller 40-seat "gourmet" Eye of the Needle section, with a $31 prix fixe, five-course menu. There was a cocktail lounge and new drive-up valet parking. The attempt was to create an entity that responded to fads, and that served all tastes, from average joe to cosmopolite.

Needle cocktails documented some of the passing trends. In 1980, after the Tut Tut cocktail, the drink menu turned tiki with beverages like Polynesian Paralysis and the Flaming Mauna Kea. By the mid-'80s, one could mellow the mood with a J.L. Seagull, a blend of lemon, vodka, and light rum. By the early '90s, a guest could be touched by a Steaming Angel, made with steamed milk and Frangelico liqueur.

Part of the tower's new populism was the Needle's experiments with becoming a kind of humorous billboard and cheerleader for major events and promotions. This goes back to at least 1971, when Paul Dorpat and John Hillding were allowed to hang a 250-foot-long cloth sculpture called the "Universal Worm" from the Observation Deck of the Needle as part of United Arts Day. The worm concept was the brainchild some years earlier of Tom Robbins. Local artists incorporated it into their work and various guerilla art "happenings" and installations in the '60s and '70s. The "worm" was striped in black and white, and looked a bit like a tiger's tail. It was soon ripped by the winds and hauled down, but it appears to have been the first whimsical inflatable placed on the Needle.

For its 20th birthday, the Needle went through a major remodel. All the old fixtures and furniture were auctioned off. It kept up its tradition of serving creative, popular-themed cocktails, like the Flaming Mauna Kea, the J.L. Seagull, and the Steaming Angel.

The restaurant was redone, and divided into two sections that offered a local, less expensive menu and a gourmet menu. The Needle wanted to attract more hometown customers.

In a 1962 comic book, Donald Duck visited the Needle and accidentally turned it into a giant pinwheel firework.

In the mid-1980s, a giant Dungeness crab appeared on the top of the Needle to promote National Seafood Week; in 1987, a 70-foot-tall inflatable King Kong was attached to the Needle for Halloween. For the Goodwill Games in 1990, to which the Needle's owners contributed an unprecedented $100,000 to become the "Official Symbol Tower," an enormous gold medal was hung around the Needle's "neck." The Needle had an inflatable basketball when Seattle hosted the Final Four in 1995, and a "Refuse to Lose" baseball during the Mariners' playoff run that same year.

Sports and animals also came together in horseracing, with the longtime Space Needle Handicap at Longacres racetrack. In 1988, readers might have been forgiven for mistaking this *Times* headline for another battle over growth: "Captain Condo Holds Off Agitated Native to Win Space Needle." Instead, horse and rider won a $30,000 purse.

The Needle also continued to be the site of various stunts, such as in 1988, when business partners Mick McHugh and Tim Firnstahl divided their legendary restaurant holdings based on a coin toss from the top of the Needle (McHugh won the silver dollar toss, which came up tails). The roof has been repainted for publicity stunts, as in 1995, when Vanna White appeared on the circular roof, repainted as the "Wheel of Fortune" to coincide with the popular game show's visit to Seattle. Many flags have flown from its mast, honoring everything from the Seahawks' 12th Man to Gay Pride. The Needle also hosted the Olympic torch in 1996.

New Year's celebrations at Seattle Center became another tradition. The Needle has hosted parties, made itself into a platform for fireworks, and substituted one of its elevators to act as the ball during televised "Times Square of the West" countdowns. The Needle, designed to be lit up, has had a long connection with fireworks. The earliest actually occurred before it was built. On April 21, 1961, marking the one-year countdown to the opening of the fair, Century 21 organizers shot off fireworks from the site of the future Needle. Skyrockets and aerial bombs exploded at around 600 feet to mark the height of the Needle-to-be. Fireworks for the opening and closing of the fair were visible from the Needle too.

In the '80s and '90s, fireworks displays on the Needle became more common and spectacular.

The Needle also began to host inflatable guests. In the mid-1980s, a Dungeness crab "climbed" to the top of the Needle for National Seafood Week.

The Needle was decked out for other events. It wore a gold medal during 1990's Goodwill Games . . .

and a banner of Gay Pride in 2011.

The top house was painted to celebrate the University of Washington Husky football team's national championship in 1991.

Later on, the Needle became a firework. This was foreshadowed in a 1962 *Walt Disney's Comic* that saw Donald Duck and his nephews visit a world's fair just like Seattle's, and klutzy Donald managed to turn the top of the Needle into a spinning fireworks pinwheel. That was more or less recreated in reality for the Needle's 25th anniversary in 1987 in a spectacular fireworks display on the top house. In 1994, the Needle began placing fireworks along the shaft and on the roof, turning it into a spectacular "giant sparkler."

In the 1980s, the KING-TV *Almost Live* comedy show cast members would help host the Needle's New Year's Eve event. John Keister had those duties for several years, even after he was involved in one of the most memorable Seattle media hoaxes, akin to Orson Welles's famous panic-inducing Martian invasion radio broadcast of the 1930s.

One evening in 1989, the KING comedy show was on at 6 p.m. instead of its usual late-night slot. It happened to be April Fool's Day, so *Almost Live* ran a spoof news bulletin

In 1995, it became the "Wheel of Fortune" when that popular game show came to Seattle.

announcing that the Space Needle had fallen over. The report included a graphic of the Needle lying in ruins on the ground. Words on the screen indicated it was "April 1st." Keister said the inspiration for this bit came from an expression he'd heard used commonly in the broadcast media when a reporter was headed out for some time off: "Unless the Space Needle falls down, don't call me."

Keister thought people might be fooled for a few seconds. Instead, a worried city overwhelmed Seattle's 9-1-1 emergency system. The Needle was deluged with some 700 calls as people clamored to know the fate of loved ones. Keister had to go back on the air and reassure people that the Needle was still standing, but not everyone got the word. "A team of doctors from Eastern Washington came over to help give humanitarian aid," he said. Higher-ups at KING were furious, as was the news department, and "the Space Needle was beyond pissed," he recounted. Apologies were issued, and Keister kept his job and was even invited back to do his Needle New Year's hosting. He had gained new respect for the power of TV. It also was a lesson in what an icon the Needle had become: newspapers around the world carried the story of the joke gone wrong.

In 1999, Seattle architecture critic Mark Hinshaw wrote that the Needle "reflects our rather goofy, light-hearted perspective on life." Part of its strength is as a reflection of Seattle character, a landmark that is quirky and knows how to make and take a joke.

That spirit was captured by country singer Kris Kristofferson during a Seattle concert in 1982. Talking to the audience, he said, "The Space Needle. Gaylord Perry. Tom Robbins. You got a lot of good stuff up here." A flying saucer tower, a major league spitball pitcher, and a hip comic novelist: what more does a city need?

"Grunge, Coffee, and the Space Needle"

The Needle didn't miss Seattle's grunge phase. The band Nirvana visited, and Kurt Cobain was featured on the cover of *Monk* magazine, shown dangling off the Needle.

As the Needle approached the actual 21st century, Seattle itself became a brand. The success of Bill Gates and Microsoft, the launch of the dot-com boom, the powerful, popular dissonance of grunge rock, the caffeinated highs induced by Starbucks' conquest of the world: all moved Seattle toward something less remote from most of America. Instead of an isolated corner, Seattle was a cultural incubator and exporter. Once known for trees, salmon, and rain, it was now a trendsetter in rock, café life, and high-tech. As a young woman drawn to Seattle from Chicago by the hype told a reporter, Seattle was "Grunge, coffee, and the Space Needle." As it reached middle age, the Needle was hip again, partly because it was unhip. In the '90s, there was little nostalgia for the *Mad Men* era; Chubby and Tubby flannel shirts were in, not skinny ties or skinny Elvis. But the Needle was offbeat and retro enough to be cool for a new generation of homegrown rockers.

In 1992, the roving publishers of *Monk*, a hipster magazine produced on the road, parked in Seattle to capture the local zeitgeist. The cover of their Seattle issue featured a computer-crafted image of Nirvana's Kurt Cobain hanging off the Space Needle.

A visit to the Needle by Nirvana really did occur in 1993. *New York Times* music writer Jon Pareles was visiting grunge's ground zero and was taken to visit the Needle by Kurt Cobain, Krist Novoselic, and Dave Grohl. In a story entitled "Nirvana, the Band That Hates to Be Loved," he described it:

> Dressed in thrift-shop shirts, fraying jeans and sneakers, the three musicians didn't act like limo-level rock stars. Lunch was micro-waved burritos at a 7-Eleven. Eventually, the band members decided to take the visitor to the city's emblematic Space Needle.
>
> On line for the express elevator, a teen-ager approached, lugging a large video camera. "Uh, um, is it O.K. if I take your picture?" he asked Mr. Cobain. The guitarist scowled; his blue eyes narrowed. "I'll kill you," he said; the teen-ager cowered. Then Mr. Cobain's face relaxed into a broad smile. "Sure, go ahead," he said.

For New Year's Eve, the Needle has become "Times Square West" with its popular annual fireworks displays.

The original gas torch was removed long ago. For special occasions, the Needle installed "legacy lights."

That teen-ager with the camera is both Nirvana's livelihood and its nightmare. The band had hoped to reach a market of intelligent iconoclasts, people who distrust bands that are too popular because if so, they must be too easy to take.

Nirvana wasn't the only grunge band with a Needle connection. In a 1992 profile of Pearl Jam in the British magazine *Melody Maker*, lead singer Eddie Vedder confessed that he once scaled the Needle's suicide-prevention mesh on the Observation Deck and stole two lights from the Needle's rim, and that one of them graced his mantelpiece. The Needle even proved to have staying power in alternative music; in the late '90s, the *New York Times*, in an article entitled "Forget Pearl Jam. Alternative Rock Lives," highlighted the work of a "progressive psychedelic" band named Space Needle.

The Needle was also reflected on film and television representing different faces of Seattle and the future. The hit TV series *Frasier* (1993-2004), starring Kelsey Grammer, a spin-off of the popular *Cheers*, found the Boston psychiatrist in Seattle as a radio host, living in a luxury downtown condo with an impossible view of the Seattle skyline and the Needle. The show wasn't filmed in Seattle until its 101st episode, in 1997. The episode featured Crane

and his brother trying to get to an event honoring Frasier at the foot of the Space Needle, where the real Mayor Norm Rice had a cameo role declaring it "Frasier Day" in Seattle.

At the less cheerful end of the spectrum was the Needle's regular appearance in the 2000-02 TV series *Dark Angel*, cocreated by James Cameron of *Titanic* fame. It starred Jessica Alba as a genetically engineered renegade whose day job was as a bike messenger in postapocalyptic Seattle. Instead of a beacon to a bright new century, the Needle was a darkened, graffiti-covered derelict, and often a roost for Dark Angel's brooding, a symbol of failed dreams.

In the 1999 film *Austin Powers: The Spy Who Shagged Me*, part of a comedy series making fun of the '60s Cold War spy genre, the Needle had been turned into the headquarters of the supervillain Dr. Evil (played by Mike Myers) and his gang. Dr. Evil had become rich investing in Starbucks and had installed a giant Starbucks sign on the Needle. He lived there along with his own barista and evil miniature clone, Mini-Me.

Taken together, the TV and movie portrayals of the 1990s and early 2000s reflected the evolution of the Needle's symbolism. The period was an economic boom and saw the sprouting of condo towers in Belltown and elsewhere, representing a kind of Frasier

For its 35th anniversary in 1997, the Needle introduced a new, short-lived mascot, Sneedle.

This 1987 painting by artist Gerald "Chip" Morse is titled "Seattle: City of the Future" and imagines a Space Needle takeover of the skyline.

Craning of Seattle as a town awash in money and yuppie sensibilities. As a comedy, *Frasier* caricatured Seattle's cultural aspirations, as the lead character was constantly having his innate pomposity punctured. For the younger generation, the future seemed more bleak: *Dark Angel* showed a near future that was the opposite of that promised by icons like the Needle, a time when the lights have been snuffed and technology is used mostly for evil. And Dr. Evil teased us about Seattle's coffee-culture imperialism. Success, we were reminded, has consequences, as well as comic possibilities.

The tradition of stunts and celebrity guests continued through the 1990s. Both Carl Sagan and Stephen Hawking visited, which showed the appeal of the Needle to these great popularizers of science. Sagan lived in Seattle while undergoing treatment for cancer at Fred Hutchinson, and while here lectured on the possibilities of extraterrestrial life. Hawking was also in town to lecture. On the other side of the culture divide, controversial TV host Jerry Springer had a group of kids to dinner at the Needle to discuss gun violence and children in 1994. His young guests told him what gang colors not to wear. There were no reports of chairs being thrown.

Craziness at the Needle did occur in a 1995 episode of Matt Groening's *The Simpsons*, "Bart Sells His Soul," in which Lisa and Bart watch an Itchy and Scratchy cartoon called "Skinless in Seattle" where Itchy cuts off the top of the Needle and impales Scratchy with it. Bart is deemed to have truly lost his soul because he doesn't find it funny.

In 1997, for the Needle's 35th anniversary, a new mascot was unveiled called the Sneedle. Unlike the Wheedle, a chubby, furry critter, Sneedle was a strange, anthropomorphic Space Needle that walked and talked with a Muppetlike mouth, but he didn't stick around for long. In 1979, the Needle had briefly served as a mascot for the Seattle Mariners when the winner of a mascot competition was a character named Spacey the Needle. One difficulty: he was not very mobile on stilts, and worse, he brought no luck to the team. The Needle was also part of the Seattle SuperSonics' logos, and is still part of the symbol for the WNBA Storm.

As the Needle approached the Millennium, many of the key players in its creation were gone. John Graham, Eddie Carlson, Howard S. Wright, Ned Skinner, Norton Clapp, and Joe Gandy had all passed before the 35th anniversary. They did not get to see the real 21st century arrive, nor the surprises it had in store. But they did see the emergence of a very different Seattle from the low-rise, provincial prefair town of 1962.

The Needle left the old century on an unprecedented note. In mid-December 1999, an Algerian named Ahmed Ressam, trained by the terrorist group al Qaida, was caught coming into the United States from British Columbia at Port Angeles, smuggling the makings of a powerful bomb in his car. It was found that he had a hotel reservation near the Space Needle, and with no clear idea yet of the would-be bomber's plans, Seattle mayor Paul Schell decided to shut down the Millennium New Year's celebration at Seattle Center, just the moment Seattle had been waiting to greet since 1962. An estimated 50,000 people were expected. The Needle was determined to go on without fear: in fact it seemed important to do so. The Needle's Millennium fireworks display went off as planned, but Seattle Center was virtually empty.

The Needle took the challenges seriously, beefing up security by installing a metal detector, adding staff, and putting in barriers at the base. Some towers in the wake of 9/11 took more extreme measures. The Transamerica Pyramid in San Francisco permanently closed its observation deck following 9/11. But the Needle was determined to carry on undeterred by terrorism. In a sense, it was in its DNA to do so.

The Needle was born in a Cold War era filled with tension as well as promise: the Cuban Missile Crisis, the building of the Berlin Wall, the budding Vietnam war, the real threat of nuclear weapons. The Needle was raised as a reaction against fear and pessimism, as a statement that the future could be bright, that even in the face of dire threats, people can envision—and make—a better world and a better city. The Space Needle reminds us of that every day.

The Needle is a backdrop for superheroes during Comicon.

CHAPTER 8

The Living Needle

"O, tell me now just what it is, what heart, what mind can make a city live?"

— From *The Spirit of Seattle*, by Harold Mansfield

It was 5:30 a.m. on September 11, 2011. A small party stood on top of the Space Needle in the dark, a huge orange moon setting in the west, its light trailing across Elliott Bay. The group included Mayor Mike McGinn, police, firefighters, some Needle staff, and local media. At the time of the attack on the World Trade Center 10 years earlier, the Needle's giant American flag was raised.

It was a moving scene, the city still asleep, the mountains wrapped in darkness. Predawn, the city lights twinkled. Without visible scenery to gauge the scale, Seattle looked smaller, an island of light surrounded by dark felt. It looked more touchable too, closer to hand. A skirling bagpipe provided the sound track, with tunes like "Sweet Alastair's Lullaby" and "Amazing Grace." There were a few words. The guests took turns raising the flag up the Needle's mast to the top, and then it was lowered to half-mast in honor of the fallen.

As the flag rose, it was whipped by wind from the north. It felt like a breeze, but it was strong enough to unfurl the flag some 600 feet in the air. The banner burst open with a flow of energy, its red and white stripes rippling, racing ribbons, as if the nation's spirit was filling it, intense, powerful, fraying its edges.

In moments such as this, one realizes that the Needle is a living thing. Not just a tower of steel to show off engineering and design prowess, not a billboard or bellwether, not only a symbol, but also an entity that both moves and is moving. It is a place that is populated, with a pulse all its own. It holds the city's joy, and grief, its future and its past. It is a being that wakes up in the morning, sleeps at night, moves through the days like all of us, never quite knowing what's in store. We bring our love, joy, and sorrows there, our hopes, our memories.

Another place where the Needle stirs with life is at the opposite end from the rooftop: the basement. The Needle has a downstairs, an underground level, and much of what makes the Needle go is there, like backstage in a theater. It's the entrance for employees—up to 270 are working at one time during the summer high season, ranging from clerks and chefs to janitors to security guards, from waiters and waitresses to elevator operators and administrators.

Opposite Page
The flag at half-mast.

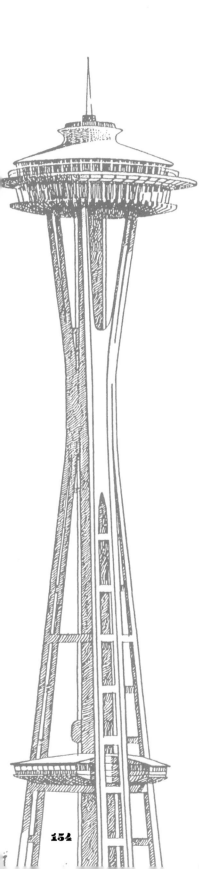

In 2002, for Century 21's 40th anniversary, the Needle went back to the future and repainted its top the distinctive "Galaxy Gold" that it had been during the fair.

The lower level is where suppliers unload at the Needle's "Red" elevator, which goes half the speed of the public ones, which are color-coded "Yellow" and "Blue." The capsule hauls salmon, coffee, toilet paper, and all the other necessities up, and brings down garbage and recycling. One odd thing about it: it has one of the best views, looking south over downtown and toward Mount Rainier. This was apparently not the original intent. During construction, an error in the plans was discovered, so the elevator that was supposed to give visitors that grandest view had to become the service elevator. On busy days, it is sometimes drafted to carry passengers too, lucky to take the slower scenic route. It must have the best view of any freight elevator on earth.

The lower level is a working level: no tourists, no glamour, no views. There are generators and pumps and employee lockers and boxes. The Needle might be famous for its upscale restaurant, special events, and high-profile stunts, but down here it is a strictly blue-collar structure for plumbers, electricians, custodians, mechanics. It feels a bit like the Needle's engine room.

Some have likened the Needle to a ship. It's an outdoor structure that holds up a five-story saucer-shaped building. The Needle must be constantly maintained, painted, have its rust scraped. A 1974 newspaper article about its long-term durability came to the conclusion that "rust is about the only natural thing that could bring the Needle down, short of cataclysm." In big storms, the slow swaying of the Needle has been said to feel like a big ship rolling gently in a heavy sea. In the 1970s, the Needle's then manager, Lee Davis, a former

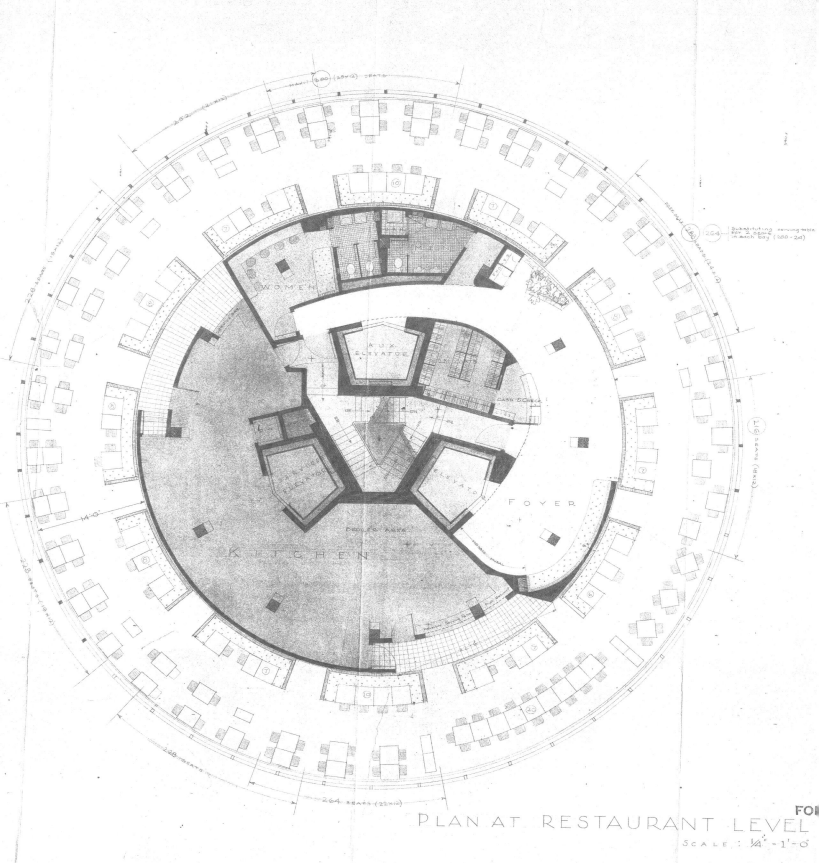

PLAN AT RESTAURANT LEVEL

SCALE : ¼" = 1'-0"

The Observation Deck was the main attraction during Century 21. The Needle owners discovered that the view was all-important. Back then, it was wide open.

The view remains the main thing: a million visitors come every year. In the '70s, for safety reasons, the outdoor deck was enclosed with mesh.

warrant officer who'd survived the attack on Pearl Harbor while serving on the battleship *West Virginia*, said maintaining the Needle wasn't a lot different from what he'd experienced in the Navy.

The Needle's utility lines run through the structure as they would a ship. The elements take a toll, especially the wet. When you're on the double-helix stairway that spirals from top to bottom in the core, you're on what is essentially a tightly wound outdoor fire escape. It's often windy, and you can hear the dull roar of the city below and the clacking of elevator cables. It's as if the city breathes through the structure. Strong winds can turn it into an instrument. In a storm, the air rushing through the Needle's core has been described as sounding like an organ note.

Diners arrive at the SkyCity restaurant and expect to eat festive food while their "ship" takes them on a circular cruise of the scenery. One 1960s reviewer described an impression that is true today: "You feel you are indeed voyaging, heading west over the Sound to the Olympics." Afterward, you can pop up to the upper deck for a stroll and some fresh air. It helps that so much of the scenery is water and mountains, an Inside Passage appetizer you can sample without ever leaving the pier. The Needle cruise is a bit faster than it used to be, but the whole world seems to have speeded up since 1962. The restaurant used to revolve once per hour, but since 2001, it takes 47 minutes to go around, roughly the length of a therapy session. Few report any motion sickness, however.

Another shiplike area is the main galley. The mezzanine level lies between the SkyCity restaurant and the Observation Deck. Most visitors pass through on stairways between the two levels, or en route to restrooms tucked in there. But the mezzanine also hides a kitchen, a small windowless office space for food-service staff, and an employee dining room where the crew eats its meals.

The top levels of the Needle are strictly utility levels, small circular spaces where the Needle engineer does his work, and one that houses elevator equipment. The Needle's engineer has a desk in an area that ought to have the greatest office view in Seattle, but there are no windows up there, only a vertical route to the roof. To get there, you climb steep stairs like those you might find on a ship, and higher up a metal ladder that takes you to a hatch that puts you on top of the Needle, save for those who need to climb up the mast to the Needle's highest point. One odd observation about the roof: it's clean up there, no bird droppings. It's apparently too high and windy for pigeons and seagulls.

Fifty years on, the Needle's Observation Deck still hums with the energy of the world's fair. It is the best place in Seattle to get a feel for what it was really like in 1962. In many ways, it's always been about the view. Gene Carlson, son of Eddie, reflected on his father's understanding after Stuttgart: "I distinctly recall my father talking about the lure of observation decks, the demonstrated willingness, no matter the location, of people to pay money to go someplace high for a view. It's a universal phenomenon, and it was an important factor in his belief that the Needle would make sense."

WORLD'S FAIR
PANORAMIC VIEWS OF SEATTLE AREA FROM THE SPACE NEEDLE

In 1962, visitors could buy a guide to the Needle's view. It contained foldout landscape paintings, like the one below looking north over Queen Anne Hill and Lake Union to Mount Baker. Note the brand-new I-5 freeway on the right.

Since 2000, the Needle has made major investments in extending access to the vista for visitors with an initiative called "Live the View." Kiosks and touch screens called SkyQ have been installed that give visitors historic and geographic information to engage with the view. More recently, stations have been added that allow folks to email digital pictures to friends and family. The Needle is in step with the social media age. Up on the top house roof, expensive live-cams have been installed so visitors using joysticks can rotate the cameras and zoom in on the cityscape while watching on a TV screen. You can't zoom in enough to be a voyeur, but you can see the living city in great detail. You not only see the view but are taken "into" it. The Needle is constantly looking to the future and was ahead of other towers in installing this 21st-century technology to advance and enhance the experience. It's a far cry from 1962, when visitors bought color foldout landscape paintings of the skyline to serve as their guide.

On the O-deck, visitors can sip soda pop from giant plastic containers shaped like the Needle while they munch on a Kobe beef hotdog or eat clam chowder. The physical experience today is very much what it was then, especially on busy summer days or holidays, when it is full of visitors from around the world. The vast majority are tourists. You hear the buzz of foreign languages and regional accents; you can watch an endless parade of people posing for pictures with the great Seattle scenery as a backdrop. There is so much curiosity about place: "Is that Canada?" No. "Where is Mount St. Helens?" It's over there, but you can only see it a few days a year. "Is that the Pacific Ocean?" It's Puget Sound; the ocean is on the other side of those mountains, the Olympics. People nod and often seem mesmerized by the view. It's hard to leave. Most Americans have never been to a world's fair (the last in North America was in Vancouver, B.C., in 1986). But this place still awakens an expo's wonder and keeps it alive.

THE EYE
OF THE
NEEDLE

SEATTLE, U.S.A.

Guests in the restaurant could refer to the back of a cocktail menu that was designed like a compass and described what was passing by outside the window during a 360-degree turn.

The Needle also lives through its owners. Most people in Seattle don't know who owns it. If you tell them the Needle is owned by members of a Seattle family, they are surprised. Many people assume it is publicly owned, but the City of Seattle and King County decided they could not risk that investment. One local booster suggested that the Port of Seattle could help pay for it by building a helipad on top, an idea that was quickly rejected.

The Eiffel Tower too started out as a private venture, but was eventually taken over by the government. But the Needle is in the hands of the extended Howard S. Wright family. Howard S. Wright Construction built the Needle, and eventually Howard S. Wright bought out the other founding partners because of his passion for it. It turned out to be a good investment. Chairman Jeff Wright said his family feels "fortunate to be the custodians of this great symbol of the city. Our stewardship is considered in our thinking. When we make a decision, we consider the financial and social implications. Will it enhance the importance of the Space Needle to the city? We want that to be our primary focus both for Seattle

The Observation Deck's SkyQ brings touch-screen technology to the Needle. Visitors can "live the view" by calling up details about the city with just the touch of a finger.

residents and for visitors." The Needle has proved to be a rarity: an icon that was locally built and is locally owned.

The Needle also continues to change. It has been continually rejuvenated. Over time, it has changed its colors, upgraded its elevators, moved its entrance, been through numerous restaurant makeovers and remodels, added the Skyline Level and Pavilion, landscaped its grounds, upgraded its Observation Deck technology. The Needle has even technically moved. In 1987, the National Oceanic and Atmospheric Administration recalculated the Needle's location with satellite technology and officially relocated the Needle 312 feet to the southwest. (That worked out to a change of 1/7000th of a degree latitude and 1/900th of a degree longitude.)

The Needle's owners have always had a stake in the success of Seattle Center, where, for example, original investors Howard S. Wright, Bagley Wright, and Ned Skinner were major supporters of the arts. The Needle ownership has supported the Monorail, and the Space Needle Corp. was a major donor to the campaign for the proposed Commons park at South Lake Union in the 1990s. The Needle, in short, is part of the fabric of a changing city, and what happens at ground level is key to what works at 600 feet in the air.

The Space Needle's owners' most recent project, the exhibition space at the Needle's base called Chihuly Garden and Glass, is designed to be a major Seattle Center attraction that brings other benefits to the campus, including the biggest permanent exhibit space for

The sights at the base of the Needle are changing too. The Wright family has created a new exhibit space, Chihuly Garden and Glass, dedicated to the work of pioneering Seattle glass artist Dale Chihuly. Ground was broken for the facility in 2011, above right.

glass artist Dale Chihuly and a children's playground for Seattle Center. For its Golden Anniversary, the Needle did not stand still. The Century 21 world's fair that gave it birth was about invention and innovation. The Needle has tried to do the same without sacrificing its essence.

The Needle also still has power as an active symbol of the Space Age, which has turned out to be very different from what was imagined half a century ago when airline companies like Pan Am took reservations for the first commercial flights to the moon. Those who

For its 50th anniversary, the Needle sponsored Space Race 2012, a contest to pick a lucky individual who will win an actual flight into orbit. The contest was announced by *Apollo 11* astronaut Buzz Aldrin, the second man to walk on the moon.

bought tickets are still waiting; Pan Am is gone, the Space Shuttle is history, and commercial space flights for the public are still in their infancy. But the private sector is taking on a bigger role in developing ways of transporting citizens into space.

For its 50th anniversary, the Needle had a competition, Space Race 2012, that would result in a grand prize winner getting a suborbital trip into space through the company Space Adventures. In the summer of 2011, the Needle brought astronaut Buzz Aldrin to Seattle to help make the announcement. For Aldrin, the second man to walk on the moon, it was his first trip to the Needle. He pronounced the view "wonderful" and compared it to a real trip into space. "You get to go up and see something that you haven't seen before," he said. Accompanying Aldrin was civilian astronaut Richard Garriott, a computer-game millionaire who had been to the International Space Station and whose father was a NASA astronaut who flew on Skylab. Garriott made this observation about space travel after his 10-day trip: "Going into space once doesn't satiate the desire." The Needle isn't a relic of a bygone age. It still resonates with the dreams of expanding humanity's horizons. It doesn't represent the end, the satiation of desire, but expresses an ongoing appetite, even among those who have been far higher than the Needle's reach.

All of which brings to mind the words of Harold Mansfield, an author who worked for Boeing and wrote an early history of the Space Needle. He reflected on the city and the fair in a prose poem he wrote called *The Spirit of Seattle*, which he sold as an illustrated chapbook to fairgoers for 75 cents. It ended with these words:

I have felt the flare of a world
at its fair—mounting the needle,
riding the monorail cars, rising
on a stair to a city in the air, flocking
the gayway, journeying to the stars.

O, tell me now just what it is,
what heart, what mind can make
a city live? Is the spirit of Seattle
a tiny seed of what America to
the world can give?

The Needle is a kind of seed that sprouted, and it has continued to regenerate over time.

In April 2011, Needle founding president Bagley Wright (second from left), the Howard S. Wright family, and other individuals and family members who played key roles in the Needle's founding gathered to commemorate the 50th anniversary of the 1961 groundbreaking.

Tower of Power

"It is America's Eiffel Tower."

— Paul Greenhalgh

In this 1962 cartoon from *Saturday Review,* the first moon walkers learn where Space Needles come from.

What is a "Space Needle"?

Eddie Carlson attached the name to his concept for a world's fair tower while he was doodling in Germany. Space was part of the fair's emerging theme, and the space race was key to Century 21's post-Sputnik funding. A needle is something sharp, pointed, but its application to tall structures comes from medieval references to classical obelisks: St. Peter's Needle in Rome, Cleopatra's Needle in London. Anyone who looked at the Stuttgart Tower would understand the reference immediately: the TV broadcast mast that inspired Carlson resembles a hypodermic.

Walt Disney predicted there would be Needles everywhere after the fair, and he was right. Such towers became almost de rigueur at expos, including San Antonio's 1968 HemisFair Tower of the Americas and Knoxville's Sunsphere in 1982. At the 1964-65 New York World's Fair, they put up Needle-inspired concrete viewing towers for the New York State Pavilion (you might remember them from the sci-fi comedy *Men in Black*). During Century 21, organizers of other fairs turned to the Needle for guidance on towers they were planning, including the never-built permanent world's fair in Miami called Interama. In 1967, an architect hired to design Interama's signature "Freedom Tower" unveiled his plan. It was Minoru Yamasaki, designer of the Needle's neighbor, the Federal Science Pavilion, now the Pacific Science Center. Yamasaki's Miami concept was a twin of the Space Needle, only set over the waters of Biscayne Bay like a Space Age lighthouse.

Post-Space Needle towers often have several common characteristics. The revolving restaurant has been copied around the world. There are now revolving dining rooms from Iraq to Iceland, offering 360-degree views and fine food in cities like Toronto, Kuala Lumpur, Macau, Seoul, Sydney, Shanghai, Tashkent, Las Vegas, Baghdad, and Auckland. Many towers have the Needle's saucer profile, and some resemble preliminary John Graham & Co. Needle designs: Calgary's sits atop a concrete shaft; Canton, China's has the hourglass shape formed by a lattice of tubes resembling drawn-together cables; the Skylon Tower at Niagara Falls, completed in 1965, looks very much like early drawings of the Space Needle.

The world was building towers millennia before the Needle came along. The Tower of Babel is described in the Bible's Book of Genesis and is perhaps the earliest symbol of global communications. It was said to have "its top in the heavens." Today there is even

Opposite Page
In its 40th-anniversary colors in 2002, the Needle once again briefly sported an orange top, but against a far different—and taller—cityscape than when it was built. Since 1962, it has been much imitated and revolving restaurants have proliferated.

The Needle was a major influence in pop culture too. The "skypads" in the TV cartoon series *The Jetsons*, launched in the fall of '62, were based on the Space Needle.

Little Elroy Jetson wore a hat similar to this Space Needle bobble beanie sold during the '62 fair. The top not only wobbles, it rattles too.

a World Federation of Great Towers. It was founded to "foster global awareness." The Needle is a member, along with the Eiffel Tower, the Empire State Building, and more than a score of others. Combined, WFGT towers host more than 40 million visitors per year.

The Space Needle influence includes tapered or flared shafts, a flying-saucer motif, exterior elevators, a revolving restaurant and observation deck, and often a Space Age name (Skylon, UFO, Sunsphere, Stratosphere). Their legacy has influenced how people see and remember cities.

The Needle also shaped how people saw the future. Perhaps no impact was greater than on a generation of children who imagined themselves living in the sky like the family in *The Jetsons*, the Hanna-Barbera TV cartoon series launched in 1962 and set in—where else?— the 21st century. The show featured Needles everywhere, even some floating in the sky. One of the cartoon's designers, Iwao Takamoto, said that *The Jetsons*' creative team took contemporary ideas and gave them a new twist. The "skypad" apartments, he said, were inspired by the Space Needle. The series debuted in September 1962, a month before the end of the Seattle World's Fair.

Joe Gandy, left, shows New York World's Fair organizer Robert Moses around the Century 21 grounds. Moses was in the middle of getting his own Space Age fair off the ground, and he wanted to see how Seattle had done.

One Seattle influence: the Needlelike observation platforms for the New York State Pavilion at Moses's 1964-65 fair.

The Jetsons embodied the "Googie" architecture of the era, a fun variant of mid-20th-century modern architecture that featured saucers, swoops, boomerangs, and rocket shapes, often along roadsides, but also in more ambitious structures. Architectural historian Alan Hess, an expert on the architecture of the era, said the Needle was "part of the exuberance and structural exploration of the times" and that it connected with the public, which more austere and less playful modern architecture often failed to do.

In assessing the Needle, Hess said, "I think the comparison to the Eiffel Tower is completely appropriate. Both were efforts to use daring engineering in an expressive manner, with the intent of taking people's breath away. They were going for a wide popular impact, and both succeeded. In looking today at the Needle, I'm impressed with how well the design stands up. A lot of these towers begin to look a bit clunky after a while, but there is a true architectural consideration for scale and proportion, particularly in those paired legs; the way the final fingers splay outward to support the disk, with the connecting curve at their base before they take off (very anthropomorphic if you look at your fingers), is elegant."

The *Washington Post*'s architecture critic, Wolf Von Eckardt, visited Seattle in the early 1970s. He was often blunt (he called the Smith Tower "a Victorian afterbirth") yet was charmed by the Needle. "The Space Needle is impressive and yet somehow cozy—just this side of kitsch and I love it."

Other experts have also judged the Space Needle a success. In their book *Towers: A Historical Survey*, a comprehensive book on the subject, authors Erwin Heinle and Fritz Leonhardt proclaimed the Space Needle "technologically and artistically a masterpiece."

In the world of international expositions, the Needle's success continues to exert influence. At an exhibition covering the history of world's fairs at Shanghai's Expo 2010, the largest world's fair ever held, millions of visitors saw numerous models and images of the Needle, which represented much more than Seattle or the Space Age, but the essence of expos themselves: forward-looking, fun, aspirational. Most international expositions attempt to create a symbol of their fair, city, and dreams. The Needle embodies the power and potential of the expo movement itself. When the expo concept debuted in China in 2010, the Needle helped to define what they are all about.

The Needle's potency lies partly in the success and prosperity of Seattle in the decades following the fair—as an exporter of planes, software, and culture, and as an importer of people and ideas. Walt Crowley captured this in his history of Seattle in the 1960s, *Rites of Passage*, in which he described the Needle as "a modernistic lingam which . . . banished the spirits of the old from the village and welcomed in the new." It is noteworthy that the neighborhoods under the Needle's umbrella, south Queen Anne near Seattle Center and South Lake Union, are shaping up as zones that embody the technology, science, and global reach symbolized by both Needle and fair.

British scholar Paul Greenhalgh, author of the superb 2011 survey of international expositions, *Fair World: A History of World's Fairs and Expositions*, concludes: "The Seattle Expo was a clear success by most yardsticks. Most of all, it contributed to the developing status of the city itself. The Space Needle, the symbol of the fair, has come to represent not only the city but also its rise and prosperity. Debatably, it is the most impressive American monument that remains from the exposition tradition: it is America's Eiffel Tower."

For the Needle to have resonance elsewhere, it must please and inspire the people who live with it every day. It must serve an authentic purpose. It must be more than a restaurant on stilts. As a civic totem, it must embody local culture in a way we can relate to and that is useful. Writer Rob Carson put it well for the Needle's 25th anniversary in 1987: "The unmistakable landmark of the Space Needle provides a reference point that is not only geographical, but temporal. It stands for a brief, shining moment of optimism, firmly anchored to the soil. That's the advantage it has over all the rest of the towers in cities around the world. It not only tells us where we are, it tells us where we've been."

A quarter of a century later, the Space Needle continues to do that. It is not frozen in 1962, though that era is part of its genetic makeup. The Needle marks our journey. It continues to convey messages about the past, present, and future. It is embedded in our language and thoughts. Scanning through the newspapers, you find that:

Opposite Page
A proposed tower for a never-built permanent exposition in Miami called Interama looks very much like the Space Needle. It was designed by Minoru Yamasaki, the Seattle-trained architect of the U.S. Science Pavilion at Century 21.

Needlelike towers have sprung up around the world, like the Pearl Tower, in Shanghai, China.

The Skylon Tower at Niagara Falls, built in 1964-65, looks very much like some of the earlier, concrete versions of the Space Needle.

In 2010, Shanghai hosted the largest world's fair in history. One exhibit displayed models of expo legacy structures, and a centerpiece was the Needle, now a symbol of world's fairs themselves.

Ivar is "as much Seattle as the Space Needle."

"You could put 1,200 Space Needles in the space in landfills saved by recycling paper and cardboard in the last 10 years."

"If these one-inch-thick [Belgian] waffles were stacked they would rise 70 times higher than the Space Needle."

"Sturgeon are so tough they could live on top of the Space Needle for a day, then return to the water and swim away."

"Mt. Walker—one of nature's 'Space Needles'—affords a spectacular view."

"[Randy] Johnson pitched like a man walking around the edge of the Space Needle, always close to a splat."

"The multiple defeats of statewide initiatives last November came as something of a shock to Seattle's political activists, who had come to believe the old political adage that from the top of the Space Needle you could see all the voters you need to win an election."

It stands for the city's memorable moments, as when baseball player Alex Rodriguez said, "When you think about the Space Needle, you also think about Junior rounding third."

It is a metaphor, a measurement, an anchor, a homing device. It literally helps us navigate the city, it lets us assess the weather and the time of day, it helps us track the course of Pugetopolis, the sprawling regional metropolitan area you can see from the Needle's top. From up there, we can watch our progress, or lack of it.

And as it reminds us of what ambitious human ingenuity and optimism can do, it also humbles us. We are still dwarfed by the ranges and waterways, the seismic, glacial, and volcanic forces that shaped our homeland. The Needle may give us, as Alistair Cooke observed, a godlike view of our surroundings, but it also reminds us that we are small. In more ways than one, it puts us in our place.

Some people who have spent a lot of time on top of the Needle express a kind of spiritual feeling that the vantage point can induce. The radio DJ Frosty Fowler, who spent six days a week watching the sun rise over the Cascades as he broadcast his morning show for several years, said that he didn't like having to come down. "God created all this," he said, sweeping his arm at the view outside the Needle's windows, "and I didn't want to miss any part of it."

It is a great lookout from which we can watch our life and times unfold. Even if one has never been to the top, its presence on the skyline tells a story each and every day, whether it seems to hover like an alien ship landing on top of Queen Anne, or has lost everything but its slender legs in the gray clouds, or catches the brilliant light of a summer sunset. Day to day, in ways great and small, it is truly "a tower unique and inspiring."

Part of the beauty and power of the Needle is how no view of it, no visit to the top, ever looks the same. It's a platform for experiencing the region, and it is a bellwether. Its appearance morphs with the winds, clouds, and light. Still, it lives on as something enduring in an evolving city.

Index

Page numbers in *italics* indicate captions and/or photographs.

Photo Credits

Front Cover: University of Washington Libraries,
    Special Collections, UW18953z
2: MOHAI 1965.3598.26.19
6: Painting by Bo Bartlett, courtesy Jeff Wright
9: PACCAR photo archive
10a: ©IgorGolovniov/Shutterstock.com
10b: ©rook76/Shutterstock.com
11-13: Space Needle archive
14: M. P. Anderson, MOHAI SHS10210
15: Linda Allen, AllensEye Photography
16: MOHAI 65.3598.26.33
17: ©1964, *The Seattle Times*
18a: Frank H. Nowell, MOHAI
    1980.7158.2.16
18b: University of Washington Libraries, Special
    Collections, UW23078
19: MOHAI 1986.5.188
20: ©Bettmann/CORBIS
21a: San Francisco History Center, San
    Francisco Public Library, AAK-0293
21b: San Francisco History Center, San
    Francisco Public Library, PUC-D3904
22: ©Bettmann/CORBIS
24: ©Depositphotos.com/kjorgen, 2011
25a: MOHAI 1986.5.43361.1
25b: PACCAR photo archive
29: NASA/VRS/Science Photo Library/
    Photo Researchers
31a: University of Washington Libraries, Special
    Collections, UW18956z
31b: John Graham & Co. Space Needle papers,
    courtesy DLR Group
32b: Courtesy Jane Carlson Williams
33a: ©ruigsantos/www.fotosearch.com
36a: University of Washington Libraries, Special
    Collections, UW31164
36b: MOHAI 1965.3598.9.54
38: MOHAI 2002.48.650
39a: University of Washington Libraries, Special
    Collections, UW31153
39b: University of Washington Libraries, Special
    Collections, UW13105
40: Harry Ransom Center, The University of
    Texas at Austin, Courtesy the Edith Lutyens
    Bel Geddes Estate
41: University of Washington Libraries, Special
    Collections, UW166855
43: MOHAI 86.5.2820.1

44: MOHAI 65.3598.9.47
45: University of Washington Libraries, Special
    Collections, UW16684
46-47: Courtesy DLR Group
48: University of Washington Libraries, Special
    Collections, UW31154
49: University of Washington Libraries, Special
    Collections, UW30034z
50: University of Washington Libraries, Special
    Collections, UW14798
51a: Courtesy Peter Steinbrueck
51b: Courtesy Peter Steinbrueck
52: John Graham, Minasian papers
53: MOHAI 65.3598.26.31
54: MOHAI 65.3598.8.42
55: University of Washington Libraries, Special
    Collections, UW18954
56: MOHAI 86.5.2802
57: MOHAI 2005.6.134
58-61: Space Needle archive
62: Painting by Irwin Caplan, courtesy
    Jeff Wright
64: Space Needle archive
65a: Minasian papers
65b: Courtesy Knute Berger
66a: Minasian papers
66b: Space Needle archive
67a-b: PACCAR photo archive
68b-69: Space Needle archive
70a: PACCAR photo archive
70b: Space Needle archive, courtesy the
    Wright family
71: Space Needle archive
72: Donald G. Moss, Space Needle archive
73: Space Needle archive
74: Painting by Jess Cauthorn, courtesy
    Jeff Wright
75a: Courtesy Jeff Wright
75b: Kenneth O. Kennedy
76: Donald G. Moss, Space Needle archive
78a: Space Needle archive
78b-81: PACCAR photo archive
82a: Space Needle archive
82b-83c: PACCAR photo archive
85: MOHAI 65.3598.26.32
87: Space Needle archive
88: MOHAI 86.5.2816
89a-90b: Space Needle archive

91: Donald G. Moss, Space Needle archive
92a-b: Space Needle archive
93a: MOHAI 2002.37.14828.1
93b: Hayley Young
94: University of Washington Libraries, Special
    Collections, UW18955
95: University of Washington Libraries, Special
    Collections, UW31156
96a: Donald G. Moss, Space Needle archive
96b: *Post-Intelligencer* Collection, MOHAI
    1986.5.3830.1
97: ©IgorGolovniov/Shutterstock.com
98: Space Needle archive
99: Painting by James Peck, courtesy Jeff Wright
101: *Post-Intelligencer* Collection, MOHAI
    1986.5.20502.1
102: University of Washington Libraries, Special
    Collections, UW31167
103: Space Needle archive
104: ©Warner Bros. Entertainment, Inc.
105a: PACCAR photo archive
105b: Courtesy Knute Berger
106: ©1962, *The Seattle Times*
107: University of Washington Libraries, Special
    Collections, UW31157
108: Hayley Young
109: MOHAI 1986.5.40799.1
111: Space Needle archive
112: Alan Pratt, ©1962, *The Seattle Times*
113: Donald G. Moss, Space Needle archive
114-116b: Space Needle archive
117: Courtesy Dean Nissen
119-120b: Space Needle archive
121: Courtesy James G. Murphy family
123a-b: Space Needle archive
125: David Rosen, SlickPix Photography
127a-b: Courtesy Dean Nissen
129a: Space Needle archive
129b: Don Wallen, University of Washington
    Libraries, Special Collections, UW31158
130: James Fiorentino
133: ©Lara Swimmer Photography
134: Tom Barlet, Space Needle archive
135: Space Needle archive
136a-b: ©Lara Swimmer Photography
137: Space Needle archive
138: ©Lara Swimmer Photography
139a: MOHAI 1965.3598.26.19
139b: Callison, Space Needle archive

141: Space Needle archive
142a: ©Disney Enterprises, Inc.
142b-143: Space Needle archive
144a: John Wiley, Space Needle archive
144b: David Mandapat, Space Needle archive
144c-145: Space Needle archive
146: Courtesy Peter Blecha
147a: Paul Gjording, Space Needle archive
147b-c: David Mandapat, Space
    Needle archive
148-9: Ross de Alessi, Space Needle archive
150a: Space Needle archive
150b: Griffin Morse ("M. Gerald")
151: Courtesy Knute Berger
152: David Rosen, SlickPix Photography
154-156a: Space Needle archive
156b: ©Lara Swimmer Photography
157: University of Washington Libraries,
    Special Collections, UW18955
158a-160: Space Needle archive
161a: David Rosen, SlickPix Photography
161b: Owen Richards Architects, Space
    Needle archive
161c: Rod Mar, Space Needle archive
162a: Space Adventures, Ltd.
162b: Rod Mar, Space Needle archive
163a: Space Needle archive
163b: Rod Mar, Space Needle archive
164: *Saturday Review*, 1962
165: David Rosen, SlickPix Photography
166a: ©Warner Bros./Getty Images
166b: Hayley Young
167a: Space Needle archive
167b: Courtesy Knute Berger
169a: ©gyn9037/Shutterstock.com
169b: ©Johan Kneisen/Shutterstock.com
169c: Urso Chappell/ExpoMuseum.com
169d: Daniel Bartush, courtesy Knute Berger
171: ©vvoe, Shutterstock.com
172: David A. Larson Jr.
173: Space Needle archive
183a: Knute Berger Sr.
183b: Kari Berger
184: University of Washington Libraries, Special
    Collections, UW18956z
Back Cover: University of Washington Libraries,
    Special Collections, UW18955

Acknowledgments

This book would not have been possible without the sponsorship of the owners and employees of the Space Needle, the folks "with their feet on the ground and their hearts in the sky." It has been an honor to tell their story, and to serve as the Needle's first Writer-in-Residence. Special thanks are due to Jeff Wright and the Space Needle's family ownership; Mary Bacarella, who saw the project through from conception to end; and David Mandapat, who made me at home at the Needle.

The Space Needle has touched literally tens of millions of lives, and I am grateful to the employees past and present, engineers, architects, Seattle World's Fair workers, scholars, collectors, reporters and broadcasters, Puget Sound residents, tourists, and scores of others, too many to name individually, for sharing their experiences. Special appreciation is due to the remarkable Jay Rockey for his ongoing assistance and wisdom.

I am grateful to the institutions and archives that have preserved so many documents helpful to understanding the Space Needle and Century 21. Thanks are due to the staff of Special Collections of the University of Washington, housing the papers of John Graham, Joseph Gandy, Edward Carlson, Ewen Dingwall, Victor Steinbrueck, and more; Greg Lange and the Puget Sound Branch of the Washington State Archives; the Seattle Public Library for its digital collection and the *Seattle Times* historical archive; public historian Lorraine McConaghy of the Museum of History and Industry; the Seattle Municipal Archives for their digital collection; Alan Michelson and staff of the Architecture-Urban Planning Library at the University of Washington; the DLR Group, keeper of John Graham & Co. architectural records; the PACCAR archives; Tammy Lau and the help of the Donald G. Larson Collection at the Henry Madden Library, California State University, Fresno; and Larry Minasian, Jennifer Trotoux, Gary Noble Curtis, and Brenda Minasian Carpenter for providing access to the private papers of the Needle's chief consulting engineer, John Minasian.

Other valuable assistance, insights, advice, and support were rendered by many others, including Bagley and Virginia Wright, George Schuchart & family, Stuart Rolfe, Gene Carlson, Jane Carlson Williams, Eugenia Woo, Jeffrey Karl Ochsner, Anne Focke, John Findlay, Alan Hess, James Gilbert, Peter Steinbrueck, Frosty Fowler, Gideon Kramer, Fred Bassetti, C. David Hughbanks, Albert Fisher, Dean Nissen, Peter Blecha, Alan Stein, Paula Becker, Rich Haag, Marie McCaffrey, Paul Dorpat, Bob Peterson, Jack Edwards, David Brewster, Joe Copeland, Rachel Hart, Kristen Russell, Steve Scher, Junius Rochester, Joe Ramsdell, Norm Bolotin, Lauren Perez Hoogkamer, Urso Chappell, Feliks Banel, Susan Roberts, Robbie Collop Anderson, John Keister, and my wife, Carol Poole.

And finally, thanks to Barry Provorse, Petyr Beck, Jon Cannell, and Judy Gouldthorpe of Documentary Media for their editing, design, and management of this amazing project.

Knute Berger
March 2012

The Author

Knute "Skip" Berger has had a lifelong fascination with world's fairs, which began when he attended Seattle's Century 21 Exposition in 1962. He remembers visiting the Smith Tower in 1961 with his Cub Scout den and seeing the still-unfinished Space Needle rising in the distance. Since then he has attended seven fairs in seven different countries as both tourist and reporter.

Berger was a longtime editor of *Seattle Weekly* and founding editor of *Eastsideweek*. He is the author of the regional bestseller *Pugetopolis*. Currently, he writes about Northwest heritage and politics for the website Crosscut, is editor-at-large and columnist for *Seattle* magazine, and is a regular commentator for Seattle's NPR affiliate, KUOW-FM. In 2008, he won the Washington State Historic Preservation Officer's Annual Media Award for his coverage of historic preservation issues. In 2011 he was named Writer-in-Residence at the Space Needle while working on this book. Berger is a Seattle native and lives in Madison Park with his wife, Carol. He is one of five generations of his family to live in the shadow of the Needle.

Knute "Skip" Berger at home in Mount Baker in the early 1960s.

At the Volunteer Park Tower, 2012.

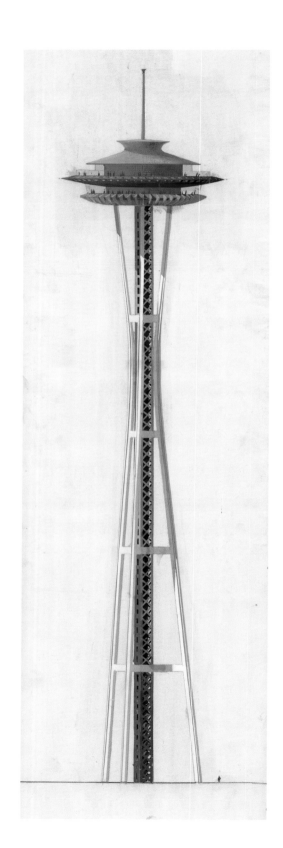

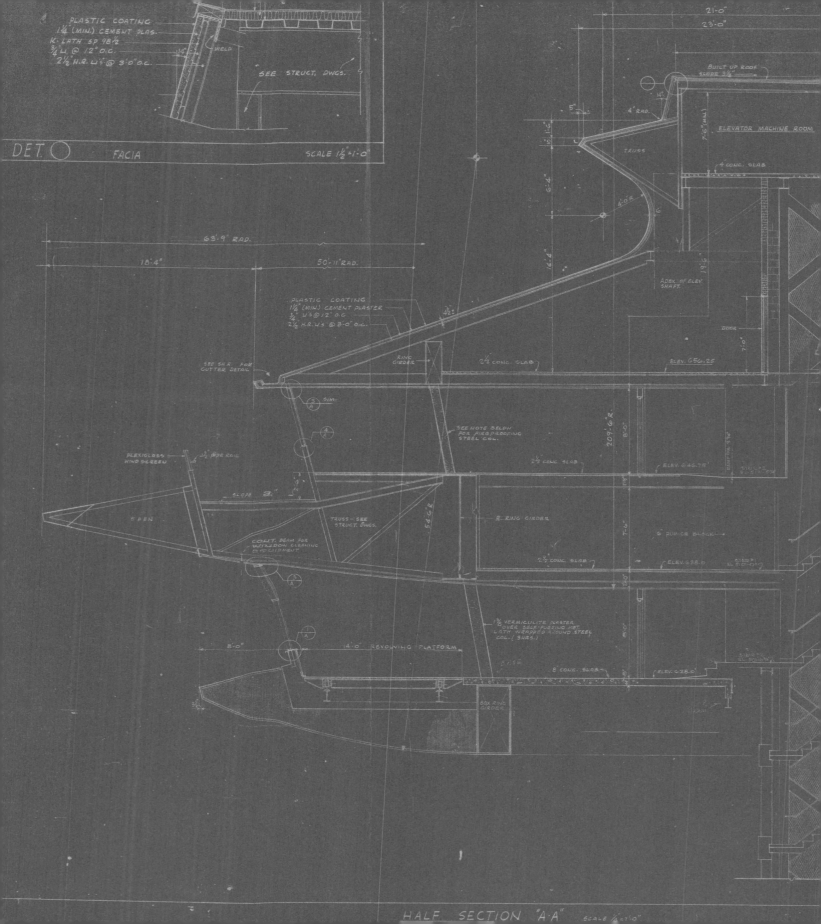

PLASTIC COATING
1¼ (MIN.) CEMENT PLAS.
K-LATH SP 98½
¾ L @ 12" O.C.
2½ H.R. L'S @ 3'-0" O.C.

WELD

SEE STRUCT. DWGS.

DET. ◯   FACIA   SCALE 1½"=1'-0"

BUILT UP ROOF
SLOPE 3½"

ELEVATOR MACHINE ROOM

TRUSS

4 CONC. SLAB

4" RAD.

5"

4" RAD.

APEX OF ELEV.
SHAFT.

DOOR

ELEV. 656.25

63'-9" RAD.

18'-4"

50'-11" RAD.

PLASTIC COATING
1½ (MIN.) CEMENT PLASTER
¾ L'S @ 12" O.C.
2½ H.R. L'S @ 3'-0" O.C.

SEE SH. R. FOR
GUTTER DETAIL

RING
GIRDER

2½ CONC. SLAB

SEE NOTE BELOW
FOR FIREPROOFING
STEEL COL.

209'-6" GR.

8'-0"

2½ CONC. SLAB

ELEV. 646.75

PLEXIGLASS
WIND SCREEN

2½ PIPE RAIL

OPEN

SLOPE 2"

TRUSS - SEE
STRUCT. DWGS.

54'-6" GR.

R. RING GIRDER

6 PUMICE BLOCK

CONT. BEAM FOR
WINDOW CLEANING
EQUIPMENT

2½ CONC. SLAB

ELEV. 638.0

1½ VERMICULITE PLASTER
OVER SELF-FURRING MET.
LATH WRAPPED AROUND STEEL
COL. (3 HRS.)

8'-0"

14'-0" REVOLVING PLATFORM

8 CONC. SLAB

ELEV. 628.0

BOX RING
GIRDER

HALF SECTION "A-A"   SCALE ⅛"=1'-0"